Global Standards and Trends

Other publications by Van Haren Publishing

Van Haren Publishing (VHP) specializes in titles on Best Practices, methods, frameworks and standards within four domains:

- IT Management
- Architecture (Enterprise and IT)
- Business Management and
- Project Management

Van Haren Publishing is publishing on behalf of leading organizations and companies: Agile Consortium, World Commerce and Contracting, IAOP, IPMA World, KNVI, PMI-NL, NLAIC and The Open Group.

Van Haren Publishing is part of the Van Haren Group and additional to the book publishing also provides the following services: accredited training materials and e-learning through Van Haren Learning Solutions, as well as independent professional certification via examination through Van Haren Certify.

Topics are (per domain):

IT Management	IT Service Management	FitSM, ISM®, ISO/IEC20000, IT4IT®, ITIL®, VerISM®, SAF, TRIM, XLA®
	Data Management	Data literacy, Data visualization, DMBOK
	IT Asset Management	HAM, ITAM, SAM
	IT Security Management	BIO, ISO/IEC27001, NIS2
	Test Management	CTAP
	Application Management	ASL
	Other	eCF, IT-CMF, Scrum
Project Management	Project Management	Half Double, ICB, ISO/IEC21500, P3.express, PM^2, PMBOK Guide, Praxis, PRINCE2
	Agile	Agile, Agile PM
	Other	PMO
Business Management	Operations Management	Lean, Lean Six Sigma, OBM, OMC, RASCI
	Contract Management	CATS CM, CATS RVM, IACCM World
	Business Information Management	BiSL, DID
	Artificial Intelligence	AI, Generative AI
	Outsourcing	OPBOK
Enterprise Architecture	Enterprise Architecture	BIAN, TOGAF
	Modeling	ArchiMate, BPMN
	Software Architecture	ISAQB
	Other	Open Agile Architecture

For the latest information on VHP publications, visit our website: www.vanharen.net.

Global Standards and Trends

6TH EDITION

Colophon

Title: Global Standards and Trends – 6th Edition
Authors: Claire Agutter, Rob Akershoek, Michiel Benda, Jan van Bon, Robert den Broeder, Andrew Campbell, Marian Carcary, Ritu Chandma, Martin Curley, Adrian Dooley, Michel Dekker, Michael Ehlers, Hans Fredriksz, Bas van Gils, Victor de Graaff, Bert Hedeman, Lex van der Helm, Dave van Herpen, Jan Heunks, Jule Hintzbergen, Wim Hoving, Andrew Josey, Declan Kavanagh, Jim Kenneally, Simon Koolstra, Mark Kouwenhoven, Bart de Lege, Alexander Lorz, Marcel Mersie, Jan-Willem Middelburg, Jan Øberg, Frank van Outvorst, Henny Portman, Nader K. Rad, Pelle Råstock, Anselm Rohrer, Arno Schilder, Ian Seward, René Sieders, Dierk Soellner, Jasper Sonnevelt, Gernot Starke, Dick Theisens, Linda Tonkes, Gunther Verheyen, Frank Wammes, Sybrand Wildeboer, XLA Institute, Anton Zandhuis, Ruben Zeegers

Publication of: Van Haren Publishing, www.vanharen.net
ISBN Hard copy: 978 94 018 1309 9
ISBN eBook: 978 94 018 1310 5
ISBN ePub: 978 94 018 1311 2
Print: First edition, first impression, May 2025
Layout and design: Coco Bookmedia, Amersfoort – NL

DREAM. LEARN. ACHIEVE.

The Van Haren Group emphasizes the value of shared knowledge and best practices to help organizations avoid redundancy and achieve success in a rapidly evolving environment. By simplifying communication and maintaining high-quality information, we advocate for the use of standards and frameworks to establish a common language and reduce errors within organizations.

Van Haren Group highlights the critical role of people in effectively applying these standards and frameworks. To support this, Van Haren Group provides accessible publications, high-quality learning solutions, and certifications designed to help professionals and students understand and apply best practices. These materials are developed in collaboration with industry experts and knowledge partners like IPMA International and The Open Group.

We are committed to investing in these areas to support professional growth and development in the years to come.

In today's age of Artificial Intelligence, Van Haren Group recognizes the transformative potential of AI technologies across industries. By integrating AI-driven solutions and insights into our offerings, we empower organizations to harness innovation, automate complex processes, and make data-driven decisions. Our resources are designed to address the challenges and opportunities posed by AI, ensuring professionals remain at the forefront of this technological evolution.

Van Haren Group highlights the critical role of people in effectively applying standards, frameworks, and AI tools. To support this, we provide accessible publications, high-quality learning solutions, and certifications tailored to bridge the gap between AI theory and practice. Collaborating with industry experts and knowledge partners like IPMA International and The Open Group, we deliver resources that integrate AI expertise with traditional best practices.

Recognizing the importance of practical skills alongside theoretical knowledge, Van Haren Group focuses on competence-based resources to foster essential skills and competencies, including those vital for AI adoption. From understanding machine learning frameworks to leveraging AI for strategic decision-making, we are committed to equipping professionals with the tools and skills necessary to thrive in the AI-driven future.
Together, we empower individuals and organizations to dream, learn, and achieve. With a foundation rooted in industry expertise, a focus on human skills, and a forward-looking approach to AI, Van Haren Group is your partner in navigating the challenges and seizing the opportunities of the digital age.

Enjoy your journey,
team Van Haren,
Ivo van Haren, CEO

Van Haren Group Portfolio

IP Distribution Van Haren Publishing has the know-how of enabling authors and communities to communicate in the form of IP Distribution. It is the main product that we distribute around the world via a complex eco-system of multiple channels. Our overall objective is to ensure that IP Distribution and the communities involved continue to grow.

Publishing Van Haren Publishing manages the publishing process from start to finish. Our extensive portfolio in the field of IT & IT Management, Enterprise Architecture, Business Management, and Project Management is a testament to the high-quality level of all our publications. For us, a publication means any content that can be delivered in the format of a hardcopy book, ebook, or ePub.

Courseware These are accredited, ready-to-give, high-quality course materials for trainers and students. Take a look at our portfolio on www.vanharen.net. Organizations only pay per candidate and can give high-quality training without having to worry about version control, revisions, accreditation, personalization, or delivery.

eLearning Van Haren Learning Solutions creates its own eLearning content. To better support our partners, we have also successfully secured access to high-quality materials

from various suppliers, enabling us to offer a diverse and comprehensive portfolio.
Created by experts, we offer everything from professional certifications to personal development. By using the latest technology, we make learning simple, engaging, and effective. Whether you're looking to boost your career or acquire new skills, Van Haren eLearning supports you every step of the way.

Exam An examination is a well-executed practice to measure if a person has mastered a level of knowledge sufficiently enough. We take away many of the challenges of doing an exam by including a free practice exam set-up in the same examination environment. Our exams can be done any-where-any-time- on any device.

Certification Van Haren Learning Solutions provides professional certification including social badge for those who passed our exams. Our exams are always backed by the communities that practice in the certifications we provide. This guarantees quality certifications, and all of our certification activities are ISO 17024 compliant.

Accreditation We can also accredit organizations and audit them. We do this to guarantee they are compliant with the quality standard to provide accredited training on a best practice governed by Van Haren Learning Solutions. Organizations are audited on their quality management system, trainers, and training material.

For more information for all these products, please visit our website: www.vanharen.net

Contents

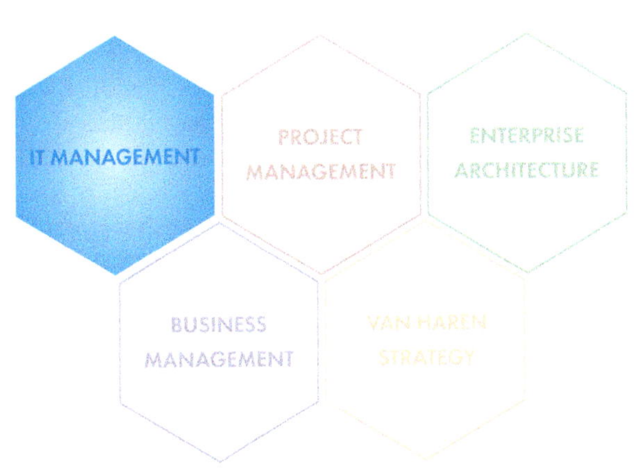
IT MANAGEMENT
PROJECT MANAGEMENT
ENTERPRISE ARCHITECTURE
BUSINESS MANAGEMENT
VAN HAREN STRATEGY

ASL®

1 TITLE/CURRENT VERSION

ASL® 3 – Application Services Library for Application Management

2 THE BASICS

ASL is the framework for application management, based on best practice. ASL provides an approach for managing and optimizing the application portfolio and life cycle of all applications, with the goal to maximize business outcome and user experience, while containing costs, reducing risk, and ensuring compliance.

The application landscape in most organizations has grown in complexity over the years, consisting of hundreds of applications delivered by a multi-vendor ecosystem covering SaaS applications and/or packaged-based software running on a private or public cloud. The challenge is to rationalize, modernize and optimize the application portfolio, reduce technology debt, as well as deliver new features faster and safer, while improving sustainability, reducing cost and ensuring compliance to an increasing number of regulatory requirements.

ASL is designed to address these challenges by providing a management framework that covers all processes for planning, developing, maintaining, and supporting applications throughout their entire life cycle, from ideation to retirement. It ensures that applications, and the entire portfolio, continue to meet the changing requirements and needs of the organization.

ASL integrates several best practices into a comprehensive application management framework, including BiSL, Agile development, DevOps and IT service management.

3 SUMMARY

ASL provides a best practice process framework covering all activities to manage the life cycle of applications and related vendors. It is designed to address a hybrid technology landscape, including SaaS, packaged software, and custom-built applications, and supports a hybrid delivery model encompassing waterfall/project delivery, Agile development, and DevOps.

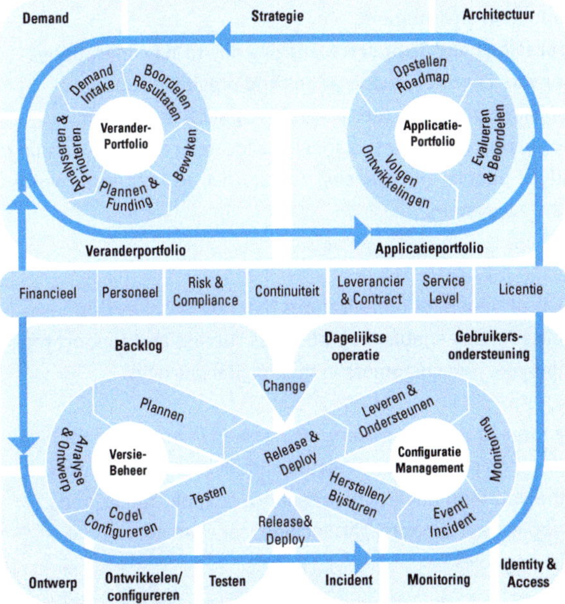

Figure: High level scheme of the ASL3 framework

The ASL framework consists of the following process clusters, as illustrated in the Figure:

Strategic Portfolio Management: Managing the portfolio of applications and initiatives (projects or epics) aligned with strategic goals and architectural roadmaps.

Develop and Maintain: Designing and configuring changes in applications (e.g., configuring SaaS or standard software packages) to fulfill new business needs or regulatory requirements, performing periodic technology upgrades, fixing issues (including security vulnerabilities), and implementing other improvements.

Connecting Processes: Coordinating change and release activities to enable controlled deployment of changes into the production environment.

Operations and Support: Managing day-to-day operations to ensure continuous operations and providing support by resolving potential issues and fulfilling service requests.

Supporting Processes: Managing allocated resources (funding/budget, people, and licenses), costs, risks, and vendors involved in the ecosystem.

4 TARGET AUDIENCE

ASL is designed for organizations that rely on many business applications to enable their business success and support their employees and customers in their digital journeys.

The target audience is everyone involved in managing the application portfolio and related initiatives/projects, involved in the development and maintenance of applications, and/or application support. This includes for example the following roles:

- Application portfolio managers
- IT managers
- Application managers and product owners
- Software developers and application specialists involved in application development (and operations)
- Application support specialists
- Business analysts
- Architects
- People involved in managing the costs, risks and compliance of applications

5 SCOPE AND CONSTRAINTS

ASL focuses on managing and optimizing the end-to-end application landscape within an organization. This includes any type of application, such as SaaS, standard software packages, and custom-built software, regardless of the delivery model, including project delivery, Agile development, and/or DevOps.

ASL manages the entire life cycle of all applications, encompassing planning, design, development, maintenance (and improvement), and continuous operations. ASL helps to rationalize and modernize the application landscape, reduce technology debt, and drive strategic change and continuous improvement.

ASL ensures that applications deliver the expected value/ outcome while managing costs, risks, and ensuring compliance.

ASL integrates well with other practices to build a comprehensive management system, including BiSL, TOGAF, ITIL, DevOps, FinOps, Cyber security, and Agile development.

6 RELEVANT WEBSITE

www.vanharen.net

ASL® 2 - Een framework voor applicatiemanagement

Language: English, Dutch

ISBN 9789087533120 (NL)

ASL® 3 Foundation (Courseware beta version)

Language: Dutch

Product code 9789401811798

ASL® 3 Foundation

Product code 04008ASL3FNLP

Baseline Informatie-beveiliging Overheid (BIO)

1 TITLE/ CURRENT VERSION

BIO2, Baseline Informatiebeveiliging Overheid

2 THE BASICS

If you work for the Dutch government, you will deal with the BIO.

3 SUMMARY

Within the Netherlands, government bodies must comply with regulations regarding the Baseline Information Security Government, also known as BIO.

The Baseline Information Security Government (BIO) was introduced as the standard framework for information security within the Dutch government. With the introduction of BIO2 in 2025, the government aligns with the European NIS2 directive, further tightening the duty of care regarding information security. BIO2 is based on internationally recognized standards such as ISO/IEC 27001 and provides an integrated framework that enables governments to effectively manage risks in an increasingly complex digital world.

In an era where information is crucial for citizens, entrepreneurs, and government organizations, BIO2 helps protect sensitive and confidential data. It offers practical guidelines to ensure continuity and security, thereby strengthening trust in digital collaboration.

4 TARGET AUDIENCE

This baseline is intended for those who work in the national government, municipalities, water boards, or provinces and are involved in the implementation or continuation of the Baseline Information Security Government. It may also be useful for those who hold a position related to it, such as government advisors or employees of organizations that provide services to the government.

5 SCOPE AND CONSTRAINTS

The BIO describes the implementation of information security and is mandatory for the national government, municipalities, water boards, and provinces.

6 RECOMMENDED READING

Implementing and handling resources:
https://www.bio-overheid.nl

BIO Self-Assessment:
https://www.cip-overheid.nl/producten-en-diensten/producten?product=BIO-SA

Baseline Informatiebeveiliging Overheid (BIO) gebaseerd op de ISO 27002:2022

Language: Dutch

ISBN 9789401810456

Certified BIO2 Professional-Foundation (CBP-F)

ISBN 9789401812773

Certified BIO2 Professional (CBP) – Baseline Informatiebeveiliging Overheid

Product code VHLSCBPBIO2FB

COBIT®

1 TITLE/ CURRENT VERSION

COBIT® 2019

2 THE BASICS

Originally designed for auditors to audit the IT organization, COBIT (Control Objectives for Information and Related Technology) is about linking business goals to IT objectives (note the linkage here from vision to mission to goals to objectives). The whole COBIT 2019 focusses on: how can your organization do governance, how does the organization keep understanding all the external reasons to exist and internal drivers to be what the organization wants to be. Additionally, COBIT identifies the associated responsibilities of the business process owners as well as those of the IT process owners.

3 SUMMARY

COBIT is owned and supported by ISACA. It was released in 1996; the current version is COBIT®2019.
The COBIT principles and enablers are generic and useful for enterprises of all sizes, whether commercial, not-for-profit or in the public sector (Figures 1 and 2).
COBIT 2019 updates the framework for modern enterprises by addressing new trends, technologies and security needs.
The framework still plays nicely with other IT management frameworks such as ITIL, CMMI and TOGAF, which makes it a great option as an umbrella framework to unify processes across an entire organization.

New concepts and terminology have been introduced in the COBIT Core Model, which includes 40 governance and management objectives for establishing a governance program. The performance management system now allows more flexibility when using maturity and capability measurements. Overall, the framework is designed to give businesses more flexibility when customizing an IT governance strategy.

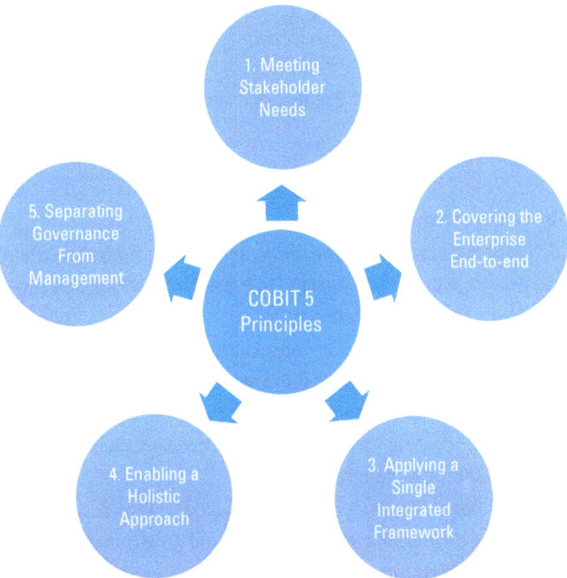

Figure 1: The COBIT® 2019 principles

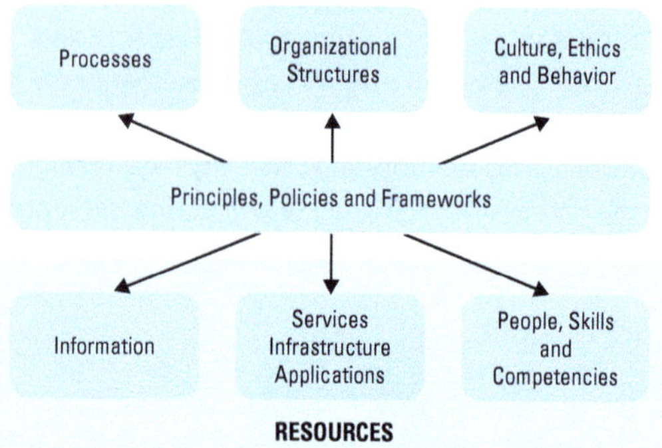

Figure 2: The COBIT® 2019 enablers

COBIT 2019 components

COBIT 2019 Framework – Introduction and methodology: The main guide that introduces the basic COBIT principles alongside the structure of the overall framework.

COBIT 2019 Framework – Governance and management objectives: A companion guide that dives into the COBIT Core Model and 40 governance and management objectives. Each objective is described including its purpose, how it connects with the enterprise and how it aligns goals.

COBIT 2019 Design Guide: A companion guide that offers in-depth guidance for developing a uniquely tailored governance system for your organization.

COBIT 2019 Implementation Guide: The fourth companion guide in the framework, which guides businesses through implementing the governance strategy once it's developed. This includes best practices, ways to avoid pitfalls and how to integrate your COBIT 2019 strategy with your COBIT 5 strategy.

COBIT principles and benefits

One major change to COBIT 2019 is that it now encourages feedback from the practitioner community. You will be able to purchase the *COBIT 2019 Design Guide*, but ISACA has also released a crowdsourced version of COBIT where practitioners can leave comments, suggest improvements or propose new concepts and ideas.

The COBIT framework is designed to be more prescriptive to guide companies in developing a governance strategy, while also allowing organizations to more comfortably tailor a unique best-fits governance strategy. It defines the "components to build and sustain a governance system: processes, policies and procedures, organizational structures, information flows, skills, infrastructure, and culture and behaviors". Formerly referred to as 'enablers' in COBIT 5, these components better define what businesses need for a strong governance system.

COBIT best suits clients that use multiple frameworks — such as ITIL, ISO/IEC 2000 and CMMI — with certain silos within IT using their own framework or standard. It's also well suited to organizations that are required to follow specific regulatory guidelines from the government and local authorities.

COBIT helps businesses align existing frameworks in the organization and understand how each framework will fit into the overall strategy. It can also help businesses monitor the performance of these other frameworks, especially in terms of security compliance, information security and risk management. It's also designed to give senior management more insight into how technology can align with organizational goals. You can directly map pain points in the business to certain aspects of the framework, emphasizing the need for 'control-driven IT'. The framework gives CIOs and other IT executives a way to demonstrate the ROI on an IT project and how it will help reach key business objectives.

4 TARGET AUDIENCE

Senior business management, senior IT management and auditors.

5 SCOPE AND CONSTRAINTS

COBIT provides an 'umbrella' framework for IT governance across the whole of an organization. It is mapped to other frameworks and standards to ensure its completeness of coverage of the IT management lifecycle and support its use in enterprises using multiple IT-related frameworks and standards.

Some strong points are:

- Value creation through effective governance, management enterprise information and technology (IT) assets
- Business user satisfaction with IT engagement and services by enabling business objectives
- Compliance with relevant laws, regulations and policies

Constraints:

- Treating COBIT as a prescriptive standard when it should be interpreted as a generic framework to manage IT processes and internal controls. Key themes from COBIT must be tailored to the specific governance needs of the organization
- Lack of commitment from top management – without their leadership and support, the IT control framework will suffer and business alignment of IT risks will not happen
- Underestimating the cultural change – COBIT is not just about the technical aspects of IT. The organization needs to have a good understanding of the governance controls for the IT risks

6 RELEVANT WEBSITE

www.isaca.org

COBIT® 5 – A Management Guide

Language: English

ISBN 9789087537012

CTAP

1 TITLE / CURRENT VERSION

CTAP 2.0 (Certified Test Automation Professional)

2 THE BASICS

CTAP is a certification scheme for enhancing the quality of test automation in the field of software projects.

3 SUMMARY

Professionals and organizations are becoming increasingly dependent on IT, which raises questions about the quality of software.

The speed at which software is developed today makes manual testing obsolete. It's not easy to keep the pace up. The speed of development and releases is important in an Agile/DevOps environment. The concepts of Continuous Integration and Continuous Delivery (CI/CD) are commonplace nowadays. Continuous testing is a need of CI/CD, where test automation plays a key role.

In this scenario, test automation extends beyond simply automating regression tests. Test automation must be implemented across the entire development process. This requires that tests must be administered as quickly as possible and, preferably, automatically. Test automation is one of the first things that is implemented within Agile teams. However, knowledge and expertise are frequently restricted to one team or project and are difficult to transfer to other teams or projects.

A too technical approach is frequently suggested, limited to a focus on tools and too little attention paid to people, organizations, data and processes. This makes it difficult to scale and transfer best practices within an organization.

The goal of CTAP is to set up test automation in a way that will be beneficial in the future so that other members of the organization can take advantage of it. Extra attention is required for the creation of test automation that is reusable, expandable, and transferable in a manner that ensures that inside the organization a reliable quality level of test automation is reached.

This demands more attention to detail and focus on transferability and knowledge sharing, but it also affects how specific test situations and test scripts are created.

Certified Test Automation professionals and organizations benefit from:

- Increasing the quality of test automation
- Reusability of test automation
- Leverage industry best practice from a vast amount of professionals over many years
- Have a common language within your team and organization in relation to test automation
- Guaranteed quality level of a test automation engineer

The result of applying for CTAP is:
"Create a common understanding of the level of expertise required for managing Test Automation".

4 TARGET AUDIENCE

The target audience for CTAP consists of everyone who is involved in the setup and development of test automation: test automation engineers, test architects and managers with the responsibility for securing test automation inside the organization.

5 SCOPE AND CONSTRAINTS

The scope of CTAP is defining the common understanding of applying test automation on the required quality level inside the organization and especially for software projects in different kinds of development methods. By hand of CTAP a required level of expertise can be granted.

Strenghts

- Offers a common language for guaranteeing the quality of test automation
- Covers all relevant aspects of test automation
- Usable in various organizations
- Supported by the CTAP consortium
- Developed and maintained by experts from the field

Constraints

- In the near future CTAP will be further developed for an advanced and expert level. For now, the foundation level is available.

6 RELEVANT WEBSITE

www.vanharen.net

Testautomatisering wendbaar organiseren

Language: Dutch

ISBN 9789401806510

Certified Test Automation Professional (CTAP) Foundation

Language: Dutch

Product code VHLSCTAPTESTB

DAMA-DMBOK

1 TITLE/ CURRENT VERSION

DAMA-DMBOK2 (Data Management Body of Knowledge), Second Edition

2 THE BASICS

DAMA-DMBOK is a comprehensive guide providing a standard, industry-view of data management functions, activities, and best practices. It serves as the definitive introduction to data management as a professional discipline.

3 SUMMARY

DAMA-DMBOK is owned and maintained by DAMA International (The Data Management Association). First published in 2009, with the current version being the Second Edition released in 2017.

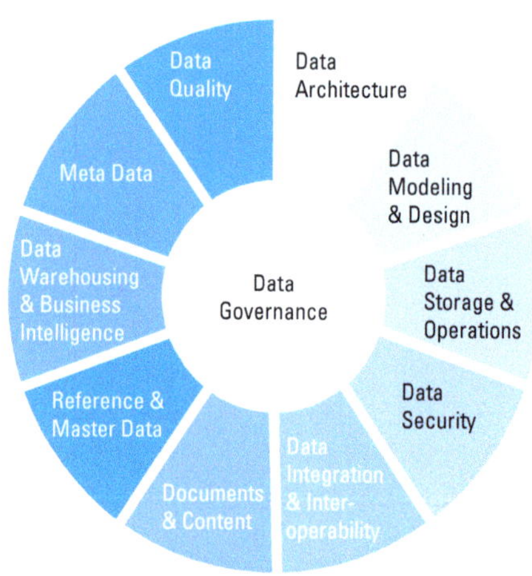

The DAMA-DMBOK framework describes data management through related Knowledge Areas centered around:

- Data Governance
- Data Architecture
- Data Modeling and Design
- Data Storage and Operations
- Data Security
- Data Integration and Interoperability
- Documents and Content Management
- Reference and Master Data
- Data Warehousing and Business Intelligence
- Metadata Management
- Data Quality Management
- Big Data and Data Science

Each Knowledge Area is described in terms of:

- Context and business drivers
- Activities and deliverables
- Tools and techniques
- Implementation guidelines
- Best practices and metrics

4 TARGET AUDIENCE

- Data management professionals at all levels
- Enterprise and data architects
- Data stewards and data governance professionals
- Database administrators and developers
- Business intelligence and analytics professionals
- Business stakeholders involved in data initiatives
- Information technology leaders
- Students and educators in data management

5 SCOPE AND CONSTRAINTS

Strengths:

- Provides comprehensive coverage of data management disciplines
- Based on real-world practitioner experience
- Vendor and technology neutral
- Supported by a global community of data management professionals
- Can be used alongside other frameworks and standards

Constraints:

- Focuses on 'what' needs to be done rather than detailed 'how-to' implementation
- Must be adapted to specific organizational contexts
- Requires interpretation and tailoring for specific industries or use cases

6 RELEVANT WEBSITE

www.dama.org

Data Management – A Gentle Introduction

Language: English

ISBN 9789401805506

Data Management courseware based on CDMP Fundamentals

Language: English

ISBN 9789401812917

eLearning Data Management based on CDMP

ISBN: 10044VHEL4113

Data Literacy

1 TITLE

Data Literacy

2 THE BASICS

Numbers are central to our understanding of performance. They enable us to make informed decisions. The way we determine success or failure is almost always based on numbers. We derive great value from the stories that numbers tell, yet we rarely consider the significance of how we use them.

Data Literacy is an umbrella term to cover all required skills to understand, work with and share data effectively. Understanding data requires a set of skills that are easy to learn, but in general are far from intuitive. None of us is born with the capacity to understand data: it is a human abstract construct, so we all need to learn how to work with it. We can learn a lot from our data to improve our processes and our lives. But before we get to the value of data, we need to get a better understanding of what data is and what it isn't.

3 SUMMARY

This training program provides a foundation for developing strong data literacy skills and advancing through the entire data lifecycle—from initial understanding to persuasive storytelling with data. It guides learners through four main topics, each building on the last to foster a well-rounded, critical, and practical approach to working with data.

Topic 1: Read Data

Learners begin by establishing a fundamental understanding of data properties and effective summarization techniques. They also learn to identify common pitfalls and ask critical questions when consuming data. Recommended readings by Jordan Morrow, Ben Jones, and Daniel Kahneman emphasize building a strong data literacy foundation and honing the critical thinking skills needed to interpret data responsibly.

Topic 2: Work with data

Moving from interpretation to manipulation, this section focuses on how data is created and structured. Learners discover differences between machine-generated and human-generated data, mandatory versus optional data, and key data quality dimensions. They also explore ideal data formats for analysis, the basics of data cleaning phases, and how to define meaningful performance measures. Guidance from Ben Jones, Stacey Barr, and other experts helps participants shape, clean, and prepare their data for meaningful analysis.

Topic 3: Analyze data

Here, learners delve into the analytical mindset. They examine how personal expectations influence the interpretation of results and review common cognitive biases and thinking shortcuts. The module introduces core analysis types and essential analytical skills, with readings from Nate Silver, Charles Wheelan, and Cathy O'Neil. At the end, participants are better equipped to apply critical thinking, leverage statistical concepts, and conduct thorough analyses that uncover credible insights.

Topic 4: Argue with data

In the final stage, learners progress to presenting their findings convincingly and ethically. They review the properties of exploration and explanation phases, learn to recognize questionable data practices (forgeries), and follow the data storytelling arc. Guided by insights from Brent Dykes and Michael Jones, participants refine their ability to craft compelling narratives and arguments supported by evidence rather than intuition alone.

In conclusion

By integrating data literacy, hands-on preparation, careful analysis, and persuasive argumentation, this training equips participants with a comprehensive skill set. Through recommended literature and a structured learning path, learners develop the confidence and competency needed to engage with data critically, transform raw information into actionable knowledge, and communicate their insights effectively.

4 TARGET AUDIENCE

The Effective Data Foundation – Data Literacy training is intended for anyone who uses data in the professional life to improve processes and performance.

Therefore, it is ideal for people for whom the concept of data is relatively new and who wish to become competent in using data. But also, for people working already in this field to strengthen their knowledge and improve their skills.

Data Literacy Practitioner's Guide

Language: English

ISBN: 9789401811316

EDF Data Literacy Professional Courseware

Language: English

ISBN 9789401809856

EDF Certified Data Literacy Professional

Language: English

Product code VHEDFDATALITB

Data Visualization

1 TITLE

Data Visualization

2 THE BASICS

Numbers are central to our understanding of performance. They enable us to make informed decisions. The way we determine success or failure is almost always based on numbers. We derive great value from the stories that numbers tell, yet we rarely consider the significance of how we present them.

Data visualization is an umbrella term to cover all types of visual representations that support the explanation, examination, and communication of data. To use visualizations effectively, we must do more than simply display data graphically. We must understand how visual perception works and then present data visually.

At the last step of the data pipeline, we make decisions based on data. After creating, cleaning, storing, managing, and analyzing it, we will present the data to facilitate taking action and making decisions based on it. To facilitate this process, we transform the numbers into data visualization with the help of graphs or tables in dashboards and reports. Anyone can easily create charts and tables, but are they effective?

Making good visualizations requires attention, knowledge, and expertise. If we pay too little attention to this last step of the production process, our data will not be successful. Otherwise, our message will come across as bad or wrong, which would be a great pity. That would be a shame because we have given a lot of care and attention to all the previous steps in the process, and in the last step, we would ruin this! To avoid this, a data visualization needs to be effective in the first place.

3 SUMMARY

This training program focuses on the end-to-end process of transforming raw data into meaningful, actionable insights through effective exploration, explanation, and visualization. It emphasizes understanding the data, structuring clear narratives, and applying visual perception principles to create impactful data stories. Each topic targets foundational knowledge and practical techniques, supported by recommendations from leading experts and seminal works in the field.

Topic 1: Explore and explain data

Participants learn how to systematically explore data and then explain it through compelling narratives. Key outcomes include understanding the characteristics of the exploration and explanation phases, identifying typical data forgeries, and following a storytelling arc to convey insights. Recommended readings by Brent Dykes, Cole Nussbaumer Knaflic, and Nancy Duarte guide learners in blending data analysis with narrative techniques.

Topic 2: Visual perception

This module introduces the fundamentals of how we perceive visual information and how that influences data interpretation. Learners will recall the key components of the human visual system, memory types, pre-attentive attributes, Gestalt principles, and systems of thinking. They will also learn about representing data accurately, distinguishing correlation from causation, and understanding the need for context. Works by Colin Ware and other resources support a deeper appreciation of the psychological and cognitive aspects of visualization design.

Topic 3: How to visualize data

Before designing any chart or table, learners are encouraged to answer the 'why' behind their data visualization. This section covers the decision-making process involved in choosing between tables and charts and determining the most effective chart types (using the CHRTTS framework). Recommended literature from Andy Kirk, Stephen Few, Alberto Cairo, Jonathan Schwabish, and Stephanie Evergreen provides guidance on selecting the right tools and techniques to clearly communicate data-driven insights.

Topic 4: Data visualization design

This topic moves from theory to practical design considerations. Key goals include recognizing the importance of visual hierarchy, understanding how to create it, and implementing fundamental building blocks of successful visualizations. Learners explore the use of color, layout, and grids to guide viewers' attention and understand essential design decisions that vary by chart type. Renowned resources from Andy Kirk, Stephen Few, Alberto Cairo, and others lend expert perspectives on clean, intuitive, and effective design.

Topic 5: Visualization workflow

This final segment focuses on the overall design process, from initial concept to final product. Participants will identify the right starting questions, sketch and iterate design ideas, and use structured methods like the Five Design Sheet approach.

Additional materials and guidance from Kieran Healy and others help solidify a workflow that ensures each visualization is both thoughtful and impactful.

In conclusion
By the end of this training, participants gain a holistic understanding of how to explore data, shape it into a narrative, leverage principles of perception and cognition, choose the right visual formats, and develop a design workflow. The comprehensive approach and expert-recommended literature equip learners with the knowledge and tools to become proficient in creating insightful, credible, and visually compelling data stories.

4 TARGET AUDIENCE

The Effective Data Foundation – Visualization training is intended for anyone who creates visualizations for an audience, like in reports, dashboards, or presentations.

Therefore, it is ideal for people for whom the concept of data visualization is relatively new and who wish to become competent in visualizing data. But also, for people working already in this field to strengthen their knowledge and improve their skills.

EDF Data Visualization Professional Courseware

Language: English

ISBN 9789401809887

Data Visualization Practitioner's Guide

ISBN 9789401811705

EDF Certified Data Visualization Professional

Language: English

Product code VHEDFDATAVISB

DevOps

1 TITLE/ CURRENT VERSION

DevOps

2 THE BASICS

Literally speaking, DevOps is a joining of development and operations. However, to understand what it truly is, some background is required on its origins. Ignited by Patrick Debois and Andrew Clay Shafer, discussing agile infrastructure at the Agile 2008 conference, it really caught fire after the first DevOps Days in Ghent one year later. Since then, tens of DevOps Days have been organized by a rapidly growing, hands-on community of IT professionals from both development and operations. It has led to a worldwide, bottom-up movement to enable a fast and resilient delivery of IT services. Along with this relevant movement automatically comes the inevitable desire to define and scope DevOps. Leading to semantic, even religious discussions, which in fact do not contribute to its goal (agility, collaboration and empathy across the IT value chain). So, without trying to ringfence it, DevOps aims at an organizational mindset for continuously improving value from the digital value chain by enabling cross-functional collaboration on process, technology and behavior level.

3 SUMMARY

Organizations worldwide have adopted Lean and Agile ways of working to cope with their current disruptive markets. Lean Startup principles are adopted by large multinational corporations, and Agile methodologies have outgrown the IT department, towards primary processes in lawyer firms, schools and construction agencies. This, however, does not say that these organizations actually bring new or adapted software to production with the required speed and frequency. Predominantly during this final step (often referred to as "the last mile") the delivery hampers. The root cause? The organization has too many silos, which are not (enough) connected.

The problem

Who hasn't seen them: IT departments where designers, developers, testers, support and operations live in splendid isolation from each other, with a minimal level of collaboration. The designers cherish their own requirements and methodologies, developers work on their code (possibly in Scrum teams), after which the results are pulled through the test factory, in order to be thrown over the operations wall at the end. Products, as delivered by the development teams (Scrum has named these "potentially shippable products", or PSP), pile up in front of operations' doorstep. By the way, using the PSP term consistently in Scrum implementation worldwide, has contributed greatly to the divergence of responsibility in the value chain. After all, from the (Scrum) developer point of view, their job was "done" once it was potentially shippable, hence on a pallet, waiting to be shipped. At that time, it still does not deliver any value at all! But the developer considered it done, as their work was done. No relation to value whatsoever.

And when these product increments are eventually implemented in a large release, it takes unacceptably long before errors can be related to their source. Integration problems don't come to the surface before the tester is running the acceptance tests. And what about customer satisfaction, if users are constantly faced with delays and unavailabilities? In short, DevOps addresses the need for higher user satisfaction, a dynamic balance between value and risks, shorter time to market, and more efficiency in the end-to-end chain through cross-functional collaboration.

The Three Ways

As beautifully illustrated in the DevOps bible "The Phoenix Project", the value IT can deliver to an organization is completely dependent on its ability to make the organization collaborate as a whole. Although the name suggests only Development (Dev) and Operations (Ops) will more closely collaborate, the essence is much broader than just that. Bringing together Dev and Ops is referred to as "DevOps Lite" (after Patrick Debois), whereas true DevOps also entails the integration of crucial roles such as the business, testing/QA and security. This holistic thinking is the first principle (The First Way) of DevOps.

Besides that, it is considered fundamental to DevOps to not only have (mostly Agile) development teams deliver "potentially shippable products", but to have the target deployment environments available as well (provisioning). Clearly this is where DevOps takes Agile implementations one step further, thereby providing the IT organization more valuable feedback (The Second Way) on the quality of the delivered products. Surely automation plays an essential role here. Without a high degree of automation, it is virtually impossible to provide and synchronize (DTAP) environments in a fast and standardized way.

Probably the most fundamental shift which is part of the DevOps way of working, is the way errors and risks are dealt with. Traditional organizations tend to have a cultural heritage where errors are being punished, hence covered up. DevOps organizations assume that errors and experiments are excellent, as they improve the organization's resilience (The Third Way).

It enhances the organizational capability to learn, moving these types of organizations towards a state of "antifragility" (Nicholas Taleb). They are known for their ability to absorb disturbances, even grow from them, and continuously adapt to changing circumstances.

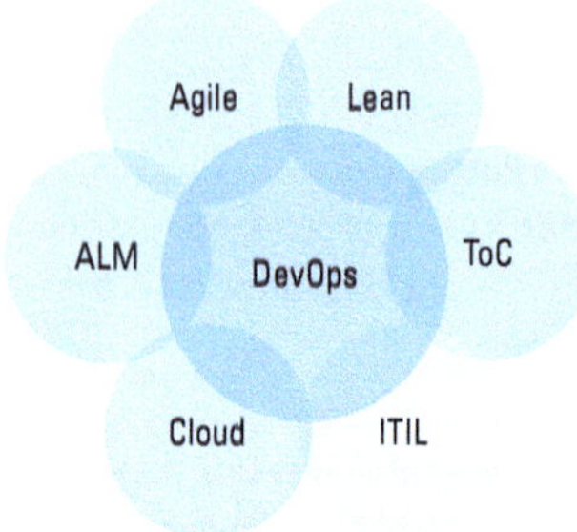

Relations

The revolutionary aspect of DevOps is not about the individual components it touches. It is the contextual combination and application of these frameworks, methods and movements. The following essential relations are identified in relation to DevOps:

Agile: Many of the principles applied in organizations that have adopted DevOps, concur with the Agile principles. Think of short feedback loops, minimizing unit size and fast flow of planned work.

Lean: The Lean way of thinking is not only applicable to the factory floor. Lean elements such as Voice of the Customer, Flow, Pull and Kaizen are used more and more in IT organizations. Waste is reduced and errors are identified and solved at the source ("no defects downstream").

Theory of Constraints: This methodology, related to Lean, is characterized by the elimination of bottlenecks. By consistently searching for essential limitations in your organization's product and service flows, these constraints (or bottlenecks) can be taken away adequately.

ITIL: Without a doubt, ITIL also plays a significant role in DevOps organizations. If well applied, the introduction of Agile and Lean principles and instruments in the entire IT delivery chain (so including operations and support) account for faster and more flexible service management processes. Take Configuration Management, which is crucial in DevOps in sharing information between several roles and domains.

Cloud: Many organizations have started their transformation to the cloud, either partly or full blown. Cloud technology enables fast provisioning, adjustment (scaling up/down) and synchronization of (DTAP) environments and in automating several build, integration, test or deployment tasks.

Themes

Typical patterns we encounter in DevOps environments include:

- **Continuous Delivery** Delivery pipelines are automated, resulting in practices like continuous integration, continuous deployment, automated testing.
- **Software Defined Anything** Servers, even entire networks are software defined nowadays. Physical, on-premise hardware is replaced by virtual machines and containers.

- **Agile architecture** Huge monolythic applications are replaced by microservices, enabling fast feedback, low regression testing and maximizing the use of market standardization.
- **Service flow** By using Lean processes, a value-driven approach challenging the end-to-end performance of the value stream, continuously optimizing batch size and queues.
- **Functional versus non-functional requirements** A sound balance between functional and non-functional system behavior requires professional product ownership, but also built-in quality, security and monitoring.
- **Learning culture** Failure is regarded as valuable learning points instead of opportunities for punishment, resulting in blameless postmortems and rewards for positive experimental behavior.

4 TARGET AUDIENCE

DevOps as a theme is relevant for everyone involved in the digital value chain. Whether you are from HR, selling mortgages, develop software, write test scripts or operate infrastructure in the cloud.

5 RELEVANT WEBSITES

Whitepaper Gene Kim:
https://www.thinkhdi.com/~/media/HDICorp/Files/White-Papers/whtppr-1112-devops-kim.pdf
Blog Rob England:
http://www.itskeptic.org/content/define-devop

DevOps – A business perspective

Languages: English, Dutch

ISBN 9789401803724 (EN)

DevOps Foundation Courseware

Language: English

ISBN 9789401803908

Experience Management (XM) and Experience Level Agreements (XLAs)

1 TITLE/ CURRENT VERSION

Experience Management (XM) and Experience Level Agreements (XLAs).

2 THE BASICS

Experience Management (XM) is an approach that guides organizations to identify, design and manage the experience they provide to their customers and employees through their services and products.

3 SUMMARY

XM is an approach that enables organizations to identify, design and manage the experience they provide through their services and products to achieve positive outcomes. XM is underpinned by three core value drivers: experience, collaboration and business impact. Through these drivers, organizations can create a win-win scenario where experience improvements benefit both the customer of the services and products and the organization itself. The primary method of managing experience is via Experience Level Agreements (XLAs). The value drivers and core concepts of XM interlinked with XLAs are visualised in the Experience Management Framework (see figure).

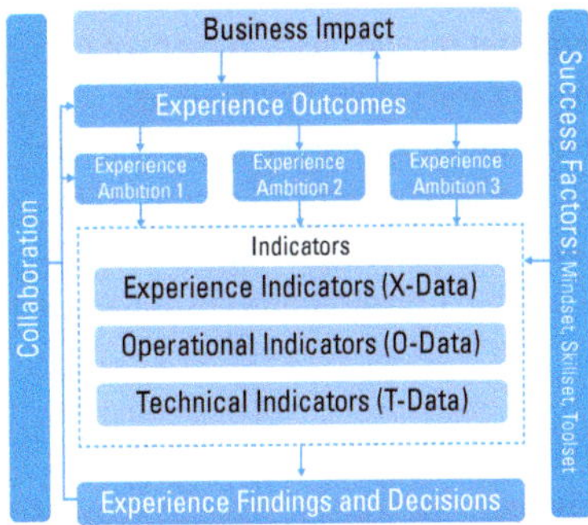

Figure: The Experience Management Framework

Providing a holistic view of how experience can be managed within an organization provides a strong foundation for understanding XM and XLAs. Collaboration, working together to successfully create win-win scenarios, and a set of three success factors influence organizational decision making as they determine the right business impacts and experience outcomes they want to make.

Following this, one or multiple experience ambitions can be created. An experience ambition forms the basis of an XLA. From here, the XM framework shifts focus to how XLAs manage experience. Through understanding the intent established in an experience ambition, organizations are guided to design and identify the relevant indicators of experience for that XLA. Indicators typically fall under three data types:

1. X (Experience) data – how people feel.
2. O (Operational) data – how the service performed. This provides context behind X data.
3. T (Technical) data – the health of technology. This also provides context behind X data.

Indicators provide an interpretation and measurement of experience that create findings and results to influence experience improvement actions and, where necessary, future adjustments to experience outcomes and/or ambitions. This ensures that XM becomes a regular process adapting to the changing experience needs of the organization's customers and employees.

XM has two certified courses:

- Experience (XLA) Foundation
- Experience (XLA) Practitioner

4 TARGET AUDIENCE

The target audience for XM consists of managers and operational delivery staff whose product or service may impact a customer or employee experience, including areas such as IT and service management, as well as managers of products, projects, operations, or HR. This is by no means a complete list. Experience is something that spans the entire organization, meaning various departments can benefit from learning XM.

5 SCOPE

XM covers how organizations can manage the experience of their customers and employees via experience level agreements (XLAs). XLAs build upon the traditional service level agreement (SLA) by incorporating sentiment of the service or product into measurement. By missing sentiment measurement, SLAs can produce the watermelon effect, where service performance is green but sentiment is red. Looking beyond SLA, metrics show the reasons behind drops in aspects like productivity and efficiency. XLAs go beyond by not just taking account of how the service is performed, but asking how the user felt about

their experience with the service. XM and XLAs are a move from measuring service-centric outputs to human-centric outcomes.

6 RELEVANT WEBSITES

https://xla.institute/
https://www.vanharen.net/standards/xla-xperience-level-agreement/
https://apmg-international.com/product/experience-collab-certification-and-training

XLA® Pocketbook
Language: English

ISBN 9789401810005

Experience Management and XLA® Foundation Courseware
Language: English

ISBN 9789401811408

Experience Management and XLA® Foundation - Online exam
Language: English

Product code VHP4001XLAFOP

FitSM

1 TITLE/ CURRENT VERSION

FitSM Version 3

2 THE BASICS

FitSM is a lightweight standards family designed for implementing IT service management (ITSM) that follows four key principles: practicality, consistency, sufficiency, and extendibility. The framework is built on seven core principles, including service- and customer-orientation, process-orientation, and continual improvement, while offering a streamlined alternative to more complex ITSM frameworks like ISO/IEC 20000 and ITIL. At its core, FitSM consists of 14 essential ITSM processes, from service portfolio management to continual service improvement, all structured to help organizations effectively plan, deliver, operate, and control IT services. The standard is maintained by ITEMO e.V., a non-profit partnership of IT management specialists, and was initially supported by the European Commission.

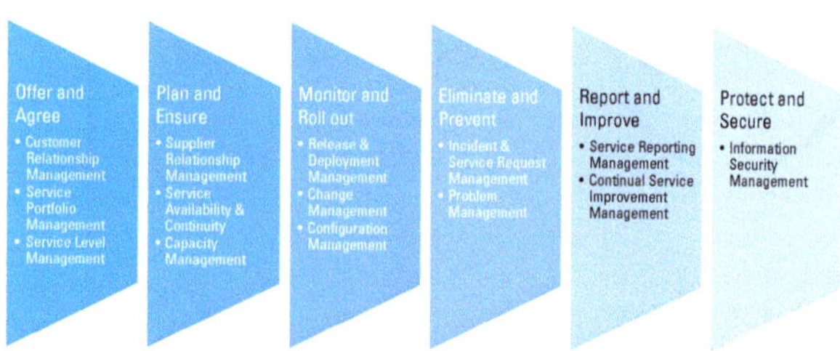

Figure: The FitSM process model

3 SUMMARY

The standard consists of multiple documents (FitSM-0 through FitSM-6) that cover various aspects from basic vocabulary to implementation guides and maturity assessment schemes:

- FitSM-0 provides a comprehensive overview of the FitSM family and establishes a common vocabulary for implementing IT Service Management across all standard parts.
- FitSM-1 provides general and process-specific requirements for implementing a lightweight IT service management system across organizations and federated scenarios.
- FitSM-2 provides recommended objectives and activities to help organizations fulfil the requirements established in FitSM-1 for effective IT service management.
- FitSM-3 provides a model of roles and responsibilities for IT Service Management implementation, describing typical roles and their relationships within organizations.
- FitSM-4 provides ready-to-use templates for ITSM documentation, while FitSM-5 offers practical implementation guides and advice for applying these templates effectively.
- FitSM-6 provides a capability/maturity assessment model to evaluate and demonstrate an organization's current ITSM capabilities and identify areas for improvement.

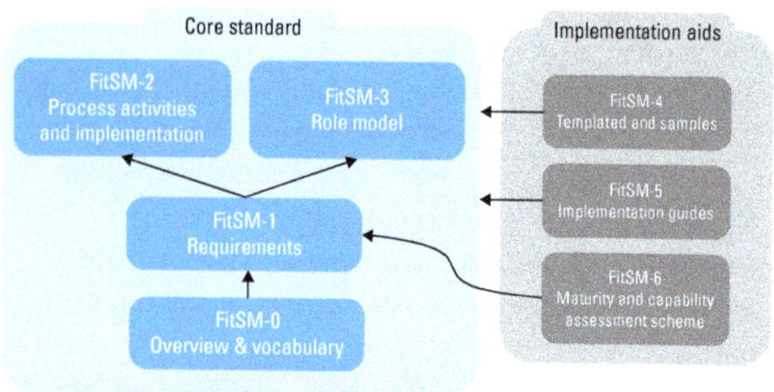

FitSM-0

At its core, FitSM-0 defines 14 essential ITSM processes, including service portfolio management, incident management, change management, and continual service improvement. The framework emphasizes three fundamental principles: service and customer orientation, process orientation, and continual improvement.

FitSM-1

FitSM-1 establishes the core requirements for implementing an IT service management system (SMS) across organizations and federated environments. The document consists of two main components: general requirements and process-specific requirements.

FitSM-2

FitSM-2 is a comprehensive document that outlines process activities and implementation guidelines for IT Service Management (ITSM). It focuses on two main areas: establishing a Service Management System (SMS) and implementing ITSM processes.

FitSM-3

FitSM-3 is a comprehensive guide that defines essential roles for implementing IT service management (ITSM). The document outlines two main categories of roles: general SMS roles and process-specific roles. Key general roles include the SMS Owner, who has overall accountability for the service management system, and the SMS Manager, who coordinates implementation and improvement efforts.

FitSM-6

FitSM-6 is a capability and maturity assessment model designed to help organizations evaluate and demonstrate their IT service management capabilities. The model enables service providers to assess their current ITSM practices against the requirements defined in FitSM-1, identifying areas for improvement and tracking progress.

4 TARGET AUDIENCE

FitSM is designed for practitioners, managers, and consultants seeking a lightweight IT service management solution. It's particularly suitable for:

- Small and medium-sized organizations requiring efficient ITSM implementation or a pragmatic approach
- Organizations new to IT service management looking for a practical starting point before investing in more comprehensive frameworks.

5 SCOPE AND CONSTRAINTS

FitSM's key strengths are:

- A lightweight, pragmatic approach built on four core principles

- Enables organizations to implement ITSM processes more quickly due to reduced complexity and focus on operationally relevant processes
- Offers a simpler, streamlined approach compared to other complex frameworks like ITIL
- Designed to be compatible with other ITSM frameworks while maintaining a more achievable implementation model
- The framework is completely free and openly accessible

The main constraints include:

- Focuses primarily on essential ITSM processes
- Requires alignment with existing organizational structures
- Primarily designed for IT service management contexts

6 RELEVANT WEBSITE

www.fitsm.eu

IT Service Management with FitSM Version 3 – Volume 1

Language: English

ISBN 9789401812528

IT Service Management with FitSM Version 3 – Volume 2

Language: English

ISBN 9789401812948

Generative AI

1 TITLE

Generative AI & Prompting

2 THE BASICS

Generative AI is a groundbreaking technology that creates new content based on what it has learned from existing content. It recognizes patterns and data from existing information. A great variety of tools are considered generative AI such as ChatGPT, Copilot, Dall-E, and Gemini. These tools are designed to make work more efficient and enjoyable by automating and enhancing content creation processes like brainstorming, reviewing documents and translation texts. The core of Generative AI lies in its ability to simulate human-like text, images, and even audio, making it a versatile solution for numerous applications.

3 SUMMARY

Generative AI, particularly in text generation, has seen rapid advancements and adoption across various sectors. This technology uses Large Language Models (LLMs), to understand and generate human-like text based on the input it receives. The principle behind these models is to predict the next word in a sequence, allowing the AI to construct coherent and contextually appropriate responses.

One prominent example is ChatGPT, developed by OpenAI, which has revolutionized how businesses and individuals interact with AI. ChatGPT, as well as Microsoft Copilot are two of many modern chatbots. The modern chatbots capabilities include text generation, translation, summarization, coding assistance, and even creative writing in all sorts of writing styles.

The revolutionary GPT models can process and understand lengthy and complex texts quickly and accurately.

Generative AI also includes tools for visual and audio content creation. Dall-E, for instance, generates images from textual descriptions, allowing users to create visual content without needing graphic design skills. Microsoft Copilot and Designer can generate new and unique images and adjust styles of existing images. Also, video content can be created with generative AI, for example by Sora, developed by Open AI, to produce realistic videos that maintain high quality and have a duration up to one minute.

Despite its numerous benefits, Generative AI is not without its challenges. Ethical concerns such as bias in AI algorithms, data privacy, and the potential for misuse in creating deepfakes or spreading misinformation are critical issues that need addressing. Moreover, the technology is still evolving, and while it can perform many tasks, it lacks genuine understanding and can sometimes produce plausible yet incorrect outputs. It is important to recognize the limitations of generative AI to fully appreciate its optimal applications.

Another key aspect of the course focuses on mastering prompting using six core principles: expert role, goal, intention, content, output format, and example output. Participants will learn how to adopt the role of an expert to provide context to the AI, define clear goals to guide the interaction, and set intentions that align with their desired outcomes. Additionally, they will explore how to craft content-rich inputs, specify the output format to meet their needs, and provide example outputs to ensure clarity. This structured approach empowers

learners to effectively communicate with generative AI and achieve optimal results.

The future of Generative AI looks promising, with ongoing improvements in model accuracy, efficiency, and applicability. The integration of AI into various domains will likely continue to grow, making it a crucial component of modern technological landscapes.

4 TARGET AUDIENCE

The target audience for the Generative AI course is everyone who wants to explore the possibilities of AI-driven creativity and communication. This includes professionals looking to enhance their workflows, such as content creators, marketers, developers, and data analysts, as well as individuals eager to learn how to effectively interact with AI through prompting. Whether you're an artist seeking inspiration, a manager aiming to optimize team productivity, or simply curious about AI's potential, this course equips you with the foundational skills and practical knowledge to leverage generative AI in your personal and professional life

5 SCOPE AND CONSTRAINTS

Generative AI's scope is vast, encompassing text, image, and audio generation. It is used in various industries, including marketing, education, healthcare, finance, and entertainment. However, the technology also faces constraints such as the need for large amounts of training data, computational resources including energy consumption, and the ongoing challenge of ensuring ethical use. Moreover, while Generative AI can simulate human intelligence to a certain extent, it is not yet capable of achieving the same level of understanding and creativity as humans.

The constraints also include the potential for job displacement due to automation, data privacy concerns, and the risk of perpetuating biases through AI-generated content. As such, it is crucial for developers and users to approach Generative AI with a focus on ethical considerations and continuous improvement to mitigate these risks.

Generative AI courseware

ISBN 9789401812795

Certified (Text) Generative AI Ambassador

Product code VHLSAICHATGTP

iSAQB Software Architecture

1 TITLE/ CURRENT VERSION

iSAQB® – International Software Architecture Qualification Board

2 THE BASICS

The International Software Architecture Qualification Board (iSAQB®) provides a comprehensive, globally recognized certification program for software architects. Through its Certified Professional for Software Architecture (CPSA®) program, iSAQB® establishes and promotes international standards for software architecture education and certification.

3 SUMMARY

The iSAQB® was established as a non-profit organization by leading industry experts, consulting firms, and educational thought leaders to develop and maintain technological standards and certifications in software architecture.
The CPSA® certification program consists of three levels:

- Foundation Level (CPSA-F®) provides fundamental knowledge and skills for software architects
- Advanced Level (CPSA-A®) offers specialized knowledge in three competence areas
- Expert Level (CPSA-E®) represents the highest certification level (under development)

The Foundation Level curriculum provides participants with the essential knowledge and skills needed to design, specify

and document software architectures for small and medium-sized systems. It focuses on understanding and executing fundamental architectural activities, including clarifying stakeholder requirements, making structural and conceptual decisions, and communicating effectively with various stakeholders. Participants learn to derive architectural decisions from system requirements and master methods for design, documentation, and evaluation of software architectures.
The training covers the core concept of software architecture, the architect's roles and responsibilities within development projects, and state-of-the-art methods and techniques.

The Advanced Level builds upon this foundation with specialized modules across three competence areas: methodical, technical, and communicative. The technical modules include topics such as Web Architectures, Service-oriented Architecture, Mobile Architectures, and Infrastructure/Cloud solutions. Methodical competence is developed through modules like Architecture Documentation, Architecture Evaluation, and Domain Driven Design. The communicative area includes modules such as Soft Skills for Architects and Requirements for Software Architects. Additional specialized modules cover areas like Safety Critical Embedded Systems, Blockchain technologies, and Evolution and Improvement of Software Architectures.

The iSAQB® does not conduct training or examinations itself but establishes training and examination regulations, accredits training organizations, and licenses independent certification bodies. This ensures high quality and standardization of software architecture education worldwide.

4 TARGET AUDIENCE

The CPSA® program serves professionals who work on solution structures in IT projects. It is particularly valuable for software architects and developers who want to enhance their architectural skills. System analysts will find the program helpful for improving communication with their development teams. Quality assurance specialists can also benefit from understanding architectural principles and their impact on system quality. The program is suitable for both experienced professionals seeking certification and those new to software architecture who want to build a strong foundation in the field.

5 SCOPE AND CONSTRAINTS

The scope of iSAQB encompasses the complete field of software architecture, ranging from foundational principles to advanced specialized domains. The Foundation Level focuses on small to medium-sized systems, while the Advanced Level extends to large-scale and complex architectures.

Strengths

- Internationally recognized certification program
- Comprehensive coverage of software architecture principles and practices
- Three-tiered certification structure allowing progressive skill development
- Independent and neutral certification process
- Strong focus on practical application and industry relevance
- Continuous updating of curricula to reflect current best practices
- International network of accredited training providers
- Over 40,000 certified professionals worldwide

Constraints

- Foundation Level scope is limited to small and medium-sized systems
- Training content focuses specifically on software architecture, not covering broader IT or development topics

6 RELEVANT WEBSITE

www.isaqb.org

Software Architecture Foundation - 2nd edition

Language: English

ISBN 9789401810425

ISM

1 TITLE / CURRENT VERSION

The ISM Method Version 5 (ISM 5)

2 THE BASICS

ISM offers a free and easy to apply ITSM solution for managing the entire IT service delivery chain. A human-centered, holistic and standardized solution focused on Customer Value and eXperience.

ISM (Integrated Service Management) is an implementable solution and differs from (or adds to) frameworks like ITIL4, DevOps, XLA, SAFe, SIAM and BiSL. All these are very valuable and correct but hard to implement and to apply due to complexity or a non-holistic coverage. Still, they offer useful insights which are integrated in ISM.

People First – The road to Customer Value is driven by people:

- the customer – provisioning and using the IT service
- the IT professional (and suppliers) – applying the ITSM practice and creating the service
- the IT leader – facilitating the professionals

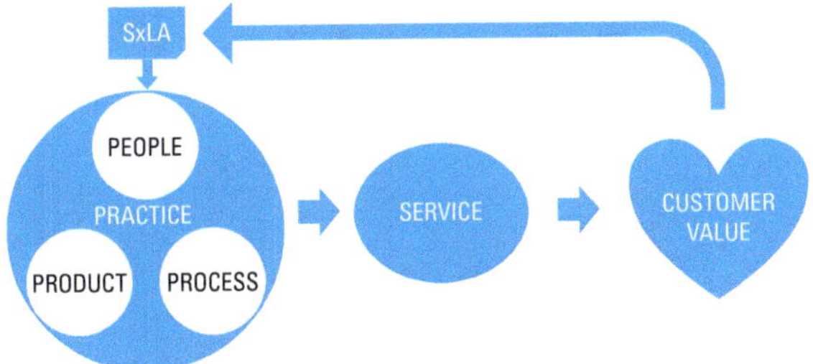

"The ISM Operating model – In applying the practice People use the Process and Product to create the services."

The challenge is not to change the people but to appreciate and use their qualities. If the ITSM solution does not deliver according to the desire of the users or can't be applied by the professionals it's not a solution, the service delivery will fail. For ISM "simplicity by design" is a hard precondition to achieve applicability. So human focus means: applicability first. The ISM Operating model organizes the mainstream of all the work, trusting on professionals to create the service, and leaders to facilitate the professionals and manage unexpected circumstances.

Holistic – In realizing Customer Value many parts and parties are involved, a missing part causes a failing system. An ITSM solution must be holistic. All levels, domains and means should be included and related (Systems Thinking). Be aware, the IT organization is bigger than the IT department, it includes the business in their role as provisioner and user, as well as the suppliers. Together they realize the service. The challenge is to get the service delivery chain on track to include all parts and parties in one way of working

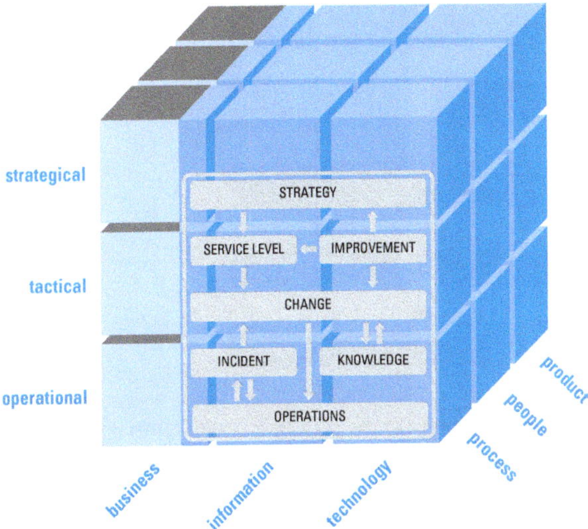

Focus on IT Services – Out-side in, the business is in charge

Traditionally, IT services are defined by 'fit for purpose' (functionality) and 'fit for use', this is about availability, performance and capacity and later on also 'easy to use' (ergonomic and intuitively). Now we learned that co-creation is also key. Services are created in continuous co-operation with customers and suppliers. To deliver and receive valuable services the focus should also be on 'fit for co-creation', as well on strategic, tactical and operational level.

In ISM the focus is on Customer Value. By definition outside-in. And the customer as Service Owner is in charge.

Standardized – IT services differ in functionality, not in quality and practices.

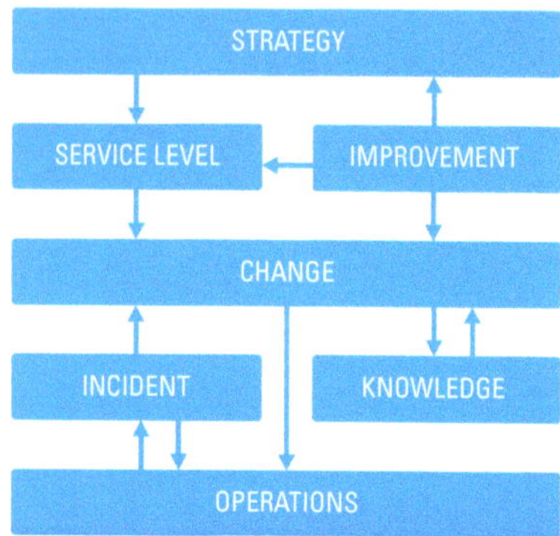

Although the content of the service may differ, this does hardly apply to the quality of the service and the way the IT services are created by the practices.

Creating services that are 'fit for purpose, use and co-creation' starts with discussing and agreeing upon the expected service, with the customers and suppliers. Followed by building, running and recovering the service when necessary. This is universal.

So the seven processes focused on customer value are fundamentally the same for all IT organizations:

1. Service Level Management – agreeing the SxLA with customer and suppliers
2. Change – designing, building and adjusting the service and the information system
3. Operations – running and monitoring the service delivery
4. Incident – recovering the service when necessary
5. Knowledge – unlock all information necessary to create the services

6. Improvement – managing risk by mitigating technical and organizational debt
7. Strategy – taking care alle necessary policies are available and practiced

Governance – Organizing the way of working, facilitating the professionals

The ISM operating model, including the process model, describes how the IT services are created. It organizes the mainstream of all the work, trusting on professionals to fill in the gaps.

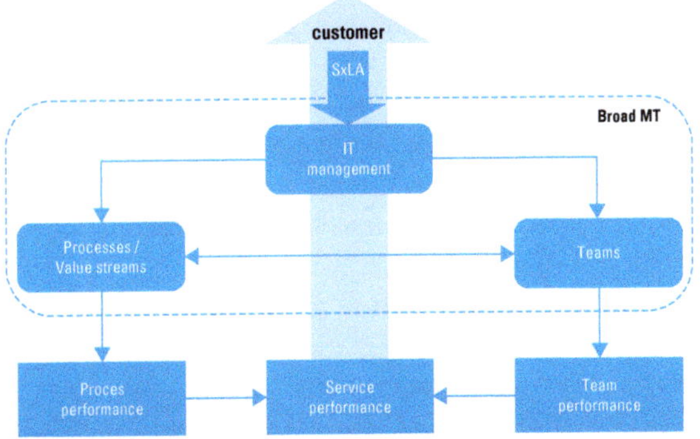

Goal of the governance is to contribute to customer value, the service performance. The management (or governance) model has two responsibilities. The first is the (phased) implementation and maintenance off the operating model, including the structured co-operation between the (internal or external) teams (people). The second is managing the operating where and when the practice and professionals needs help. In the ISM management model the performance of the teams and processes are NOT the goal, but contribute to the service performance.

Organizational change – Improving and professionalizing the IT organization is an organizational change. It's a change from process to practice, from product to service, from output to outcome, from theory to solution.

3 SUMMARY

ISM is focused on creating customer value for people by people. Value that is experienced by the user and the customer, created by the professionals and facilitated by the leaders. Applicability is the most important precondition of every successful ITSM solution.

The most important elements of ISM are:

- A clear vision on creating Customer Value
- The ISM operating model – describing the practice, including a compact process model
- The ISM management model – organizing and managing the ISM Operating model
- A complete list of clear definitions

The ISM method is a free to use and continuously evolving method. It offers an easy to apply solution for the way of working for all IT organizations and integrates the latest developments in modern IT Service Management. ISM integrates the basics of:

- Systems thinking, Simplicity by Design, Human centered Design
- ITIL4©, DevOps, BiSL, Experience Management (XLA)
- Organizational Behavior Management (OBM), Humanizing IT™

Applying ISM offers IT organizations a complete, compact and easy way of working. For those IT organizations that still feel the need to detail their way of working it can act as a platform on which they can connect and expand to more specialized methods like DevOps, ITIL, XLA, BiSL, OBM, Humanizing IT™, RASCI.

"Complexity kills the Service, real experts simplify."

4 TARGET AUDIENCE

Although the ISM Method offers a universal Service Management solution that is suitable for Enterprise Service Management, the main focus is on IT service management:

- IT managers
- Team managers
- Process managers
- IT professionals
- ITSM consultants
- ITSM trainers

5 SCOPE AND CONSTRAINTS

Strengths:

- Free to use – read the book and apply, additional information on ISM
- Suitable for all IT service organizations focusing on customer value and people
- Easy to apply Operating model and Governance model
- Clear roles and responsibilities
- Holistic from Business – IT department to IT suppliers
- Phased approach – grow within your capacity to change
- Global online training and examination on foundation level available
- Available in English and Dutch

Constraints:

- Main focus on service-driven organizations
- Leadership is required (supported but not included)
- Not suitable for micro management

6 RELEVANT WEBSITES

a. **www.ismportal.com for additional information on the ISM Method**

b. **www.servitect.nl for access to additional support and tools**

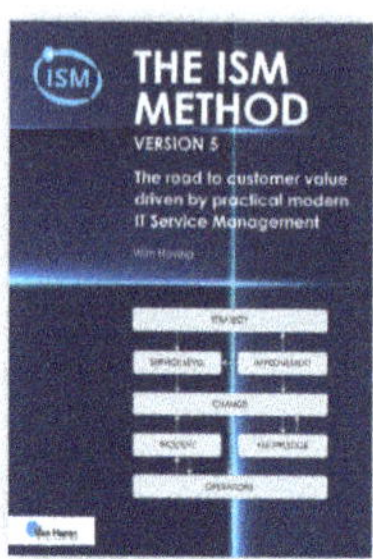

This book is the official core book for ISM5

Languages: Dutch, English

ISBN 9789401811255 (EN)

Courseware for the ISM 5th Edition Foundation exam.

Languages: Dutch, English

ISBN 9789401810791 (EN)

Certified ISM 5 Foundation (CISM5) Exam – English

Language: English, Dutch

Product code VHLSISM5ENFOO

IT Asset Management

1 TITLE/CURRENT VERSION

IT Asset Management (ITAM)

2 THE BASICS

The basics of IT Asset Management are brought together in the book *IT Asset Management Foundation*. This book provides a comprehensive introduction on IT Assets and specifics of their management. It is written for anyone that wants to start in the IT Asset Management area, either holistically or with focus on a particular stream according to which IT Assets are to be managed. It also describes how ITAM practice is linked to ITSM practices, how it is interfaced to non-IT processes and who are typical stakeholders for each specific stage of IT Asset Management process. Besides the ICT security specific topics attention is given to the organization and governance of IT security, including people, technology, and processes essential for the security of corporate assets. The book is on purpose not very technical; everyone should be able to understand it.

3 SUMMARY

The purpose of *IT Asset Management Foundation* is to describe all essential areas of IT Asset Management and also builds a solid foundation for further study of its components on advanced level. It provides also references to the ISO 19770 standard and ITIL 4. In this latest release of ITIL, IT Asset Management became one of its practices. The book covers the following areas:

- IT Asset Management Introduction
- Hardware Asset Management Introduction
- Software Asset Management Introduction
- Service & Cloud Asset Management Introduction

- People & Information Asset Management Introduction
- IT Asset Management Interfaces Introduction

The book provides a comprehensive and holistic approach on IT Asset Management, with emphasis on each stage of the lifecycle of an IT Asset and the stakeholders involved. Having IT Assets under the control is an important pre-requisite to spend IT budget in an effective and efficient manner, supports overall compliance as well as supports the compliance risk – both in the Software and Hardware area can have serious impact on company operation and reputation. A very good starting point for further specialisation in the very broad area of information security areas of expertise – namely the Software Asset Management and Hardware Asset Management.

The book *IT Asset Management Foundation* contains, besides the theoretical concepts, also practical examples.

4 TARGET AUDIENCE

- **Managers –** who are primarily responsible for implementing and governing IT Asset Management or its part in their organizations
- **IT professionals –** that need a basic understanding of ITAM or are directly involved in some of the ITAM practices (e.g. SAM Manager).
- **Procurement professionals –** that are involved in IT Assets sourcing
- **Internal audit –** as compliance is a key concept across IT Asset Management.
- **Executives** – who are primarily responsible for developing and/or approving an IT Asset Management strategy and then

overseeing its implementation and governance (The "C" suite of Corporate Officers)

- **Academicians, graduate and upper-level undergraduate students** – who must teach and master a fundamental understanding of IT Asset Management.
- **Everyone within an organization** – who wants to know more and understand the impact of IT Asset Management.

5 SCOPE

The book *IT Asset Management Foundation* covers the various areas of IT Asset Management that are also addressed in the ISO 19770 and ITIL 4, by explaining the basic concepts and technologies used and giving practical examples based on practical everyday examples

6 RELEVANT WEBSITE

www.itam.org

IT Asset Management Foundation (ITAMF) Workbook Second Edition

Language: English

ISBN 9789401807166

IT Asset Management Foundation Courseware Bundle

ISBN 978940180698B

ITAMOrg

ITAM FOUNDATION

Van Haren

ITAM Foundation exam

Language: English

Product code VHLSITAMFORGB

IT-CMF

1 TITLE/ CURRENT VERSION

IT-CMF™ (Information Technology Capability Maturity Framework™)

2 THE BASICS

Organizations, both public and private, are constantly challenged to be increasingly more agile, innovative and value-adding. CIOs are uniquely well-positioned to seize this opportunity and adopt the role of business transformation partner, helping their organizations to grow and prosper with innovative, IT-enabled products, services and processes. To succeed in this, however, the IT function needs to manage an array of inter-dependent but distinct disciplines.

In response to this need, the Innovation Value Institute, a cross-industry international consortium, developed the IT Capability Maturity Framework™ (IT-CMF™).

3 SUMMARY

The IT Capability Maturity Framework™ (IT-CMF™) represents a suite of capabilities (see Figure 1) that help improve the management of IT to deliver higher levels of agility, innovation and value creation.

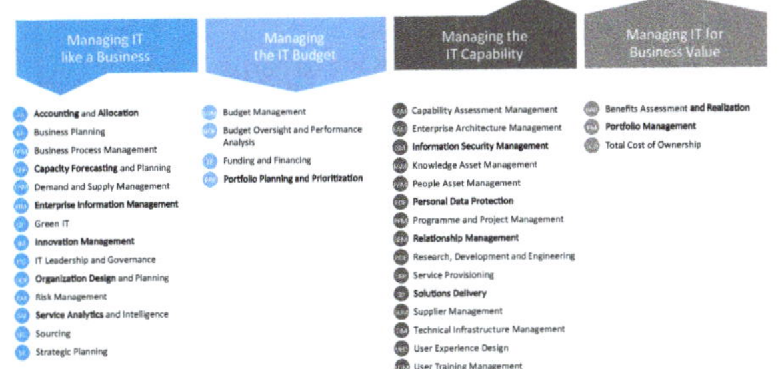

Figure 1: IT-CMF's critical capabilities

Each critical capability of IT-CMF consists of capability building blocks (CBBs), which are characterized by maturity levels, are evaluated by maturity questions and are improved by practices-outcomes-metrics (POMs). Figure 2 graphically illustrates the relationship amongst IT-CMF's principal components.

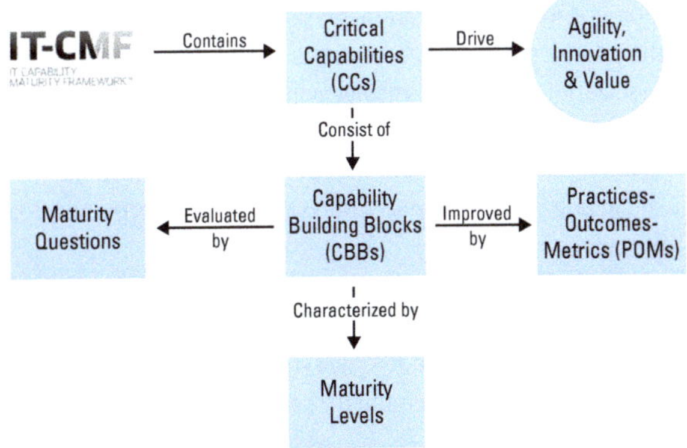

Figure 2: IT-CMF's principal components

4 TARGET AUDIENCE

Business and IT professionals seeking to harness the full potential of information technology in their organizations, including CxOs, transformation change managers, IT strategy planners, general managers, and IT professionals aspiring to demonstrate leadership in adopting better approaches to managing technology for agility, innovation and value impact.

5 SCOPE AND CONSTRAINTS

Strengths

IT-CMF is:

- An integrated management toolkit covering more than 30 management disciples, with organizational maturity profiles, assessment methods, and improvement roadmaps for each.
- A coherent set of concepts and principles, expressed in business management terms, that can be used to guide discussions on setting goals and evaluating performance.
- A unifying (or umbrella) framework that complements other, domain-specific frameworks already in use in the organization, helping to resolve conflicts between them, and filling gaps in their coverage.
- Industry/sector and vendor independent. IT-CMF can be used in any organizational context to guide performance improvement.
- A rigorously developed approach, underpinned by the principles of Open Innovation and guided by the Design Science Research methodology, synthesizing leading academic research with industry practitioner expertise.

Considerations when using IT-CMF in your organization

- IT-CMF should be adopted at a senior management level, not just at the front-line staff/practitioner level, to realize the framework's full advantages.
- The framework delivers value through change. Committing to the required organizational change will help ensure expected outcomes are achievable.
- Appropriate capability selection and setting of maturity targets benefits from an appreciation of IT-CMF's critical capabilities, as well as a blended view across an organization's business strategy, IT posture and industry context.

6 RELEVANT WEBSITE

http://www.ivi.ie

IT-CMF – A Management Guide – Based on the IT Capability Maturity Framework™ (IT-CMF™) 2nd edition

Language: English

ISBN 9789401801966

ITIL®

1 TITLE/ CURRENT VERSION

ITIL® 4 (Information Technology Infrastructure Library)

2 THE BASICS

ITIL® is the most widely accepted approach to IT service management in the world; it focuses on aligning IT services with the needs of the business.

3 SUMMARY

ITIL was created in the 1980s by the UK government's CCTA (Central Computer and Telecommunications Agency) with the objective of ensuring better use of IT services and resources.

ITIL is now owned by AXELOS: the current version is ITIL 4 (published February 2019), which updates ITIL v3/2011.

ITIL focuses on aligning IT services with the needs of the business and is supported by quality services from a wide range of providers including examination institutes, accredited training providers and consultancies, software and tool vendors. ITIL provides a structured approach to one of the most important support domains for modern business: the provision of information technology services for the improvement of business results. The new ITIL 4 guidance supports modern ways of delivering value in a co-creation effort of stakeholders, using an Agile approach in a customer-focused setting. This supports modern technologies, including DevOps and cloud computing. Its holistic approach not only supports the management of IT services, but now also supports other

domains, enabling the integration of IT with the business and with other support domains.

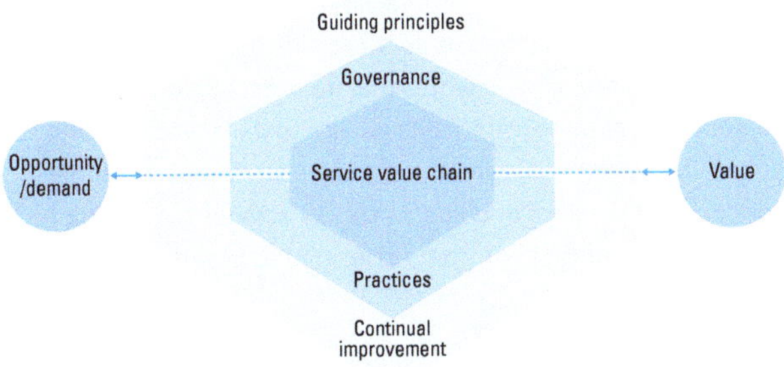

Figure 1: The ITIL 4 service value system

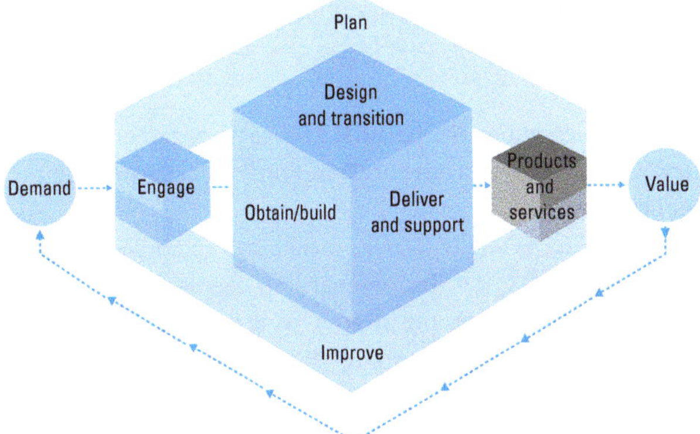

Figure 2: The ITIL 4 service value chain

4 TARGET AUDIENCE

IT service providers and IT professionals in a wide range of roles.

5 SCOPE AND CONSTRAINTS

The ITIL service value system (Figure 1) is a model demonstrating how all the components and activities of an organization work together to facilitate value creation through IT-enabled services. The ITIL service value chain (Figure 2) is a set of interconnected activities that an organization performs to deliver a valuable product or service to its consumers and to facilitate value realization. It provides an operating model for service providers that covers six key activities, applying practices to continually improve the enabled values.

Strengths

- Universally accepted as the good practice guidance for IT service management, with process and service focus
- Supported by a vast community of ITIL practitioners, gathered around itSMF (IT Service Management Forum)

Constraints

When implementing ITIL-based IT service management processes in an IT provider organization, the most common pitfalls are:

- Narrow focus on the IT unit's technology and process perspectives to gain incremental improvements; the organization should be embarking on a radical transformation journey to run IT as a business
- Failing to do an assessment before implementing ITIL practices; identifying how the current organization structure compares to the ITIL framework and the changes that will be needed to the organization and its culture
- Short term expectations; it is not a quick fix, achieved with just a handful of personnel trained and the purchase of some ITIL tools

6 RELEVANT WEBSITE

www.axelos.com

ITIL® 4 – A Pocket Guide

Language: English, Dutch

ISBN 9789401804394

ITIL® 4 Foundation Courseware – English

ISBN 9789401803939

NIS2

1 TITLE/ CURRENT VERSION

NIS2 (Network and Information Security Directive)

2 THE BASICS

To strengthen cyber security across Europe, the European Parliament voted in 2022 to adopt the revised Network and Information Systems Directive 2022/0383, more commonly referred to as "NIS2". Understanding the implications of the NIS2 Directive for an organization is challenging and best. A structured approach and understanding of cyber security and risk management is essential for organizations to become compliant.

3 SUMMARY

NIS2 is a Directive which will directly impact over 100,000 organizations in Europe. Indirectly, there are many more organizations around the globe that will be confronted with and required to address the implications of this Directive and the subsequent laws in each of the EU member states.
With 46 articles, 144 recitals, and over 140 references to other European and national legislations, the Directive requires organizations that fall under its scope to have a thorough understanding of its rules and intentions.

4 TARGET AUDIENCE

The NIS2 Directive is primarily aimed at any members of management bodies that have to address cyber security in their role in the organization and information security officers.

5 RELEVANT WEBSITE

www.euoci.eu

The NIS2 Navigator's Handbook

Language: English

ISBN 9789401811276

NIS2 Professional (CNIS2) Courseware

Languages: English, Italian

ISBN 9789401811880 (EN)

CNIS2 Professional

Language: English

Product code 43CNIS2EUOCIP

Certified NIS2 (CNIS2)

ISBN: 10043VHEL1492

SAF

1 TITLE/ CURRENT VERSION

Service Automation Framework (SAF)

2 THE BASICS

Service Automation – the concept of delivering services through smart technology – is a rapidly growing area of interest for most organizations. Companies such as Spotify, Netflix and Uber (whom deliver 100% automated services) have proven that organizations can achieve rapid growth and gain a competitive advantage by relying on Service Automation.
Since Service Automation is a new topic, there has not a lot of (practical) information available on how organizations can set up Service Automation in their organizations. The Service Automation Framework® provides a step-by-step approach that illustrates how organizations can digitize their service offering in a methodical way. The corresponding certification scheme was developed for individuals and teams who aim to demonstrate their proficiency in the methodical steps of the Service Automation Framework. Additionally, the certification scheme provides a consistent starting point for organizations who want to start digitizing their service offering.

3 SUMMARY

The Service Automation Framework consists of six main building blocks that can be divided into the 'heart' (focused on design) and the 'brain' (focused on delivery), which are both equally important in delivering automated services:

1. **User:** The building block that defines the key characteristics of the groups of people a service provider aims to serve;
2. **Service Design:** The business function that designs and defines the service offering of a service provider. It is

the concretization of the service concepts into an actual design, including the relevant support structures and digital interfaces;

3. **Technology:** The building block that defines the setup and usability of the digital interfaces, connecting service providers with their users;
4. **Automated Deployment:** The processes that enable a user to start using a service based on his or her own action;
5. **Service Delivery Automation:** The processes that enable a user to change or resolve any aspect of the service based on his or her own action;
6. **Serendipity Management:** The processes that facilitate a planned and continuous approach in order to constantly exceed the expectations of users.

Each of the six building blocks form an essential step in design and delivery of automated services.

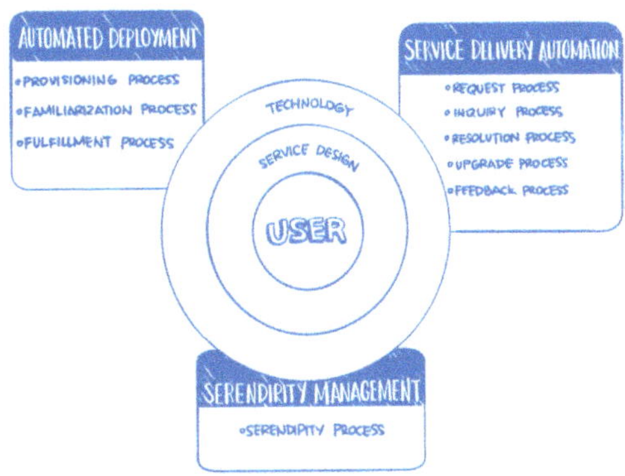

In addition to the six building blocks of SAF, the seven Service Automation Framework Techniques can be considered as a step-by-step plan that organizations can use to adopt Service Automation. Each of the seven SAFTs discuss in detail what techniques an organization should use to design and deliver automated services:

1. **SAFT1 – Building User Groups and User Characteristics:** In order to deliver 'valuable' services, it is necessary to understand the Service Perception of individual users. SAFT 1 provides the techniques to build the User Groups and User Characteristics that shape the Service Perception.
2. **SAFT2 – Translating User Profiles into User Action:** In order to ensure that services meet or exceed user requirements or expectations, service providers need to understand the needs and triggers that initiate service requests. SAFT2 provides the techniques to translate User Profiles into User Actions, keeping in mind the psychographic criteria that determine the overall UX.
3. **SAFT3 – Compose the Service Automation Blueprint**: The SAF Canvas enables the composition of a Service Automation Blueprint which outlines the 'ultimate User Experience' for a specific service and a specific User Group.
4. **SAFT4 – Technology Interface Modeling**: The goal of Technology Interface Modeling is to design a Self-Service Portal (e.g. the technology interface) based on industry best practices.
5. **SAFT5 – Implement Automated Deployment Processes:** The goal of this exercise is to apply the three processes of Automated Deployment (Provisioning Process, Familiarization Process and Fulfilment Process) into your own organization.

6. **SAFT6 – Implement Service Delivery Automation Processes**: The goal of this exercise is to apply the five processes of Service Delivery Automation (Request, Inquiry, Resolution, Upgrade and Feedback Process) into your own organization.
7. **SAFT7 – Surprise your user with Serendipity Management:** The goal of this exercise is to apply Serendipity Management to transform your organization's customers into long-term fans.

Through the chapters of the Service Automation book, each of the seven Service Automation Framework Techniques is illustrated using the case study of the Swan Hotel Group.

4 TARGET AUDIENCE

Service Automation is a growth market across the entire world. Whereas the competition in traditional Service Management products is fierce, the SAF product allows training organizations to showcase their innovative spirit and the opportunity to claim a part of the Service Automation market in their respective regions.

The Service Automation Framework is primarily intended for individuals and organizations in the service industry, who can gain a competitive advantage by digitizing their existing service portfolio. Examples of industries that the SAF is especially suitable for include the Finance, Insurance, Healthcare and Government sectors.

5 SCOPE

The Service Automation Framework book covers the necessary steps to digitize the service offering of organizations and provides guidance on the 7 Service Automation Framework Techniques.

The key benefit of the book and corresponding certification is that it provides knowledge and practical tools that can be used in practice after reading the book.

6 RELEVANT WEBSITE

http://www.apmg-international.com/en/qualifications/SAF

This book is the official core book for SAF.
Service Automation Framework
Language: English

ISBN 9789401800624

Service Automation Foundation Courseware
Language: English

ISBN 9789401802062

Scrum

1 TITLE/CURRENT VERSION

Scrum

2 THE BASICS

Scrum is an Agile framework for the iterative, incremental development of complex products, services and projects.

3 SUMMARY

Scrum employs an empirical process — a process implementing regular inspections and adaptations—for the iterative, incremental development and delivery of products, service and projects. Scrum is the leading Agile method that was originally formalized for software development, but works well for any complex, innovative scope of work.

Why is it called Scrum?
Jeff Sutherland and Ken Schwaber inherited the name 'Scrum' from the paper The New New Product Development Game of Takeuchi and Nonaka, published in 1986 in the Harvard Business Review. With the term 'Scrum', the authors referred to the game of rugby as an analogy to stress the importance of self-organized teamwork in achieving success in the 'game' of new product development.
Source: **Scrum - A Pocket Guide *(Gunther Verheyen)***

The Scrum Guide is the official Body of Knowledge for Scrum. It is maintained by Ken Schwaber and Jeff Sutherland, co-creators of Scrum. The current version of the Scrum Guide was released in November 2020.
Scrum defines how to organize work in short cycles called Sprints, see Figure.

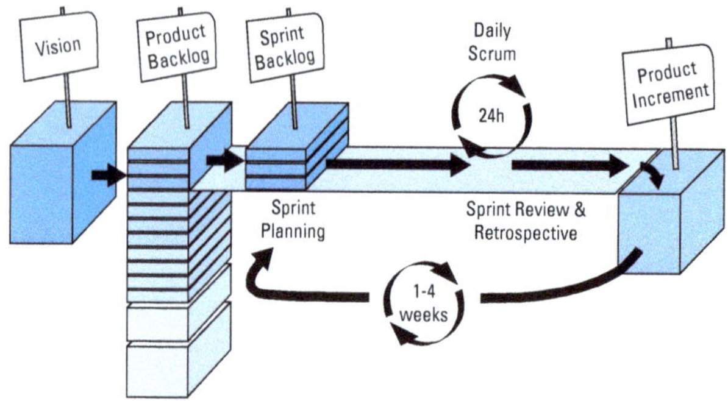

Figure: Overview of a Scrum Sprint

A Sprint's duration is never more than four weeks and typically takes one to four weeks.
Scrum defines following accountabilities within a Scrum Team:

- 'Product Owner' is a one-person player role to connect consumers, stakeholders and Scrum Teams.
- 'Scrum Master' is a one-person player role to assure that the rules of the game are known and understood.
- 'Developers' is the team of people turning functions and solutions from the Product Backlog into Done Increments.

Scrum defines following activities to happen:

- A Product Owner orders envisioned product functions and solutions in a Product Backlog.
- At Sprint Planning, the Scrum Team discusses and selects the work from the Product Backlog deemed most needed and feasible for the Sprint in order to create an actionable work plan for that selection, the Sprint Backlog.
- On a daily basis, at the Daily Scrum, the team of Developers discusses the progress toward the Sprint Goal in order to identify the most important upcoming Sprint work.

- At the Sprint Review, the Scrum Team and its stakeholders discuss the Increment(s) produced in order to identify the most important work for the next Sprint(s).
- At the Sprint Retrospective, the Scrum Team discusses how the current Sprint went in order to identify the envisioned way of working for the next Sprint.

The Scrum Master fosters and facilitates an environment where the above happens.

4 TARGET AUDIENCE

Any member of a Scrum Team or anyone involved in the adoption of Scrum.

5 SCOPE AND CONSTRAINTS

The scope of Scrum was originally intended for software development, but it is now also used for managing any kind of complex work.

Strengths

- Productivity increases (depending on team, experience, tools, environment, organizational impediments, etc.)
- Minimized time-to-market via frequent releases
- Continuous improvement and openness for changes
- Improved relationships between teams, stakeholders and customers
- Increasing engagement of co-workers

Constraints

- The need for automation and modern development tools, practices and environments

- Does not work well if organizational culture emphasis individual specialization and performance over collaborative, cross-functional collaboration
- Willingness to revise, add and improve work, management, people and organizational practices around Scrum.
- The shift from managing individuals to managing the environment

6 RELEVANT WEBSITES

- **www.scrum.org**
- **www.scrumalliance.org**
- **www.scrumguides.org**

Languages: English, Dutch, German, French

Scrum – A Smart Travel Companion

ISBN 9789401812214 (EN)

VeriSM™

1 TITLE / CURRENT VERSION

VeriSM™

2 THE BASICS

Every organization is a service provider in today's market. Even organizations selling products need to add a level of service to them. Think of banking, insurance, civil services, but also the myriad of online shops where the physical product is a commodity and the service is the distinguishing characteristic of the organization. How do we best manage our services and keep our consumers happy? Recent years have seen an explosion of different service management practices, leaving organizations confused about the best way forward. VeriSM is a new approach to help you create a flexible operating model that will work for you, based on your desired business outcomes. VeriSM describes how an organization can define its service management principles, and then use a combination of management practices to deliver value.

VeriSM describes a service management approach which is:

- **V**alue-driven
- **E**volving
- **R**esponsive
- **I**ntegrated
- **S**ervice
- **M**anagement

3 SUMMARY

VeriSM describes a service management approach from the organizational level, looking at the end-to-end view rather than focusing on a single department. Based around the VeriSM model, it shows organizations how they can adopt a range of management practices in a flexible way to deliver the right product or service at the right time to their consumers. VeriSM allows for a tailored approach depending upon the type of business you are in, the size of your organization, your business priorities, your organizational culture – and even the nature of the individual project or service you are working on.

Rather than focusing on one prescriptive way of working, VeriSM helps organizations to respond to their consumers and deliver value with integrated service management practices.

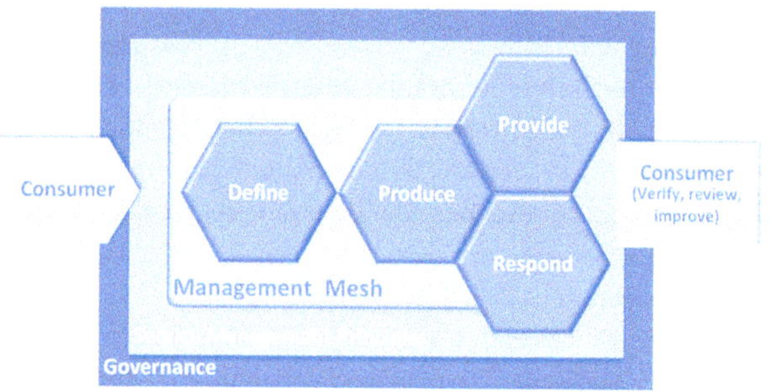

Figure: The VeriSM model

In the model, governance overarches every activity, keeping a strong focus on value, outcomes and the organization's goals. Service management principles are then defined for the organization. These act as guardrails, to make sure that all products and services are aligned with the needs of the organization. Principles will be defined for areas including security, risk, quality and use of assets, and then communicated

to all of the staff who are involved with the development and operation of products and services.

The unique element of the VeriSM model is the management mesh. This provides a flexible approach that can be adapted depending on the requirements for a particular product or service. The mesh includes:

- Resources
- Environment
- Emerging technologies
- Management practices

For each product or service, these areas are considered and the mesh is flexed where necessary.
Let's take an example. A bank wants to create a mobile application that will let users send money to their friends with just one click. The mesh for this product could include agile development practices to get rapid feedback about the new product. The bank can use its capabilities and work in innovative ways, but they must still recognise the service management principles associated with security and risk.

4 TARGET AUDIENCE

VeriSM is essential reading for anyone who works with products and services. It will be of particular interest to:

- Managers – who want to understand how to leverage evolving management practices
- Service owners and service managers – who need to bring their skills up to date and understand how service management has changed
- Executives – who are accountable for effective service delivery

- IT professionals
- Graduates and undergraduates – who will be joining organizations and who need to understand the principles of service management
- Everyone within a service organization

5 SCOPE

VeriSM includes:

- Service culture
- Organizational context
- People/structure
- Service management challenges
- Processes, tools and measurement
- The VeriSM model
- Operating in a world of digital transformation
- Selecting and integrating management practices
- Progressive management practices including Lean, DevOps and Agile
- The impact of technology on service management
- Getting started

6 RELEVANT WEBSITE

www.verism.global

VeriSM - A Service Management Approach for the Digital Age

Language: English

ISBN 9789401802406

VeriSM™ - Foundation Courseware

Language: English

ISBN 9789401802628

IT MANAGEMENT
PROJECT MANAGEMENT
ENTERPRISE ARCHITECTURE
BUSINESS MANAGEMENT
VAN HAREN STRATEGY

Agile

1 TITLE/ CURRENT VERSION

Agile

2 THE BASICS

Originating from the world of IT where the concept of Agile refers to a set of software development methods based on iterative and incremental development, where requirements and solutions evolve through collaboration between self-organizing, cross-functional teams. Nowadays, the principles of the Agile approach are also used in other domains, for example design & engineering, product development, manufacturing, etc.

3 SUMMARY

Incremental software development methods have been traced back to 1957. 'Lightweight' software development methods evolved in the mid-1990s as a reaction against 'heavyweight' methods, which were characterized by their critics as a heavily regulated, regimented, micromanaged, waterfall model of development. Supporters of lightweight methods (and now Agile methods) contend that they are a return to earlier practices in software development.

Early implementations of lightweight methods include Scrum (1993), Crystal Clear, Extreme Programming (XP, 1996), Adaptive Software Development, Feature Driven Development, DSDM (1995, called DSDM-Atern since 2008), and the Rational Unified Process (RUP, 1998). These are now typically referred to as Agile methods, after the Agile Manifesto.

The Agile Manifesto was written in February 2001, at a summit of independent-minded practitioners of several programming methods.

Manifesto for Agile Software Development
We are uncovering better ways of developing software by doing it and helping others do it. Through this work we have come to value:
Individuals and interactions over processes and tools
Working software over comprehensive documentation
Customer collaboration over contract negotiation
Responding to change over following a plan

That is, while there is value in the items on the right, we value the items on the left more.
Source: agilemanifesto.org/

The Agile Manifesto has twelve underlying principles:

1. Customer satisfaction by rapid delivery of useful software
2. Welcome changing requirements, even late in development
3. Working software is delivered frequently (weeks rather than months)
4. Working software is the principal measure of progress
5. Sustainable development, able to maintain a constant pace
6. Close, daily co-operation between business people and developers
7. Face-to-face conversation is the best form of communication (co-location)
8. Projects are built around motivated individuals, who should be trusted
9. Continuous attention to technical excellence and good design
10. Simplicity
11. Self-organizing teams
12. Regular adaptation to changing circumstances

Agile methods break tasks into small increments with minimal planning and do not directly involve long-term planning. Iterations are short time frames. Team composition in an Agile project is usually cross-functional and self-organizing and team size is usually small (5-9 people). The Agile method encourages stakeholders to prioritize "their requirements on the basis of business value".

The Agile approach is supported by the Agile Alliance, a not-for-profit organization that wants to see Agile projects start and help Agile teams perform. It is funded by individual memberships, corporate memberships, and by the proceeds from the Agile conferences. It is not a certification body and does not endorse any certification programmes.

4 TARGET AUDIENCE

Anyone involved in an Agile development project team; including analysts, architects, developers, engineers, testers and business customer/users; anyone supporting or managing an Agile project team who requires a detailed understanding of the practices and benefits of Agile development.

5 SCOPE AND CONSTRAINTS

Applicable to development environments. Improved quality; higher productivity; positive effect on business satisfaction.

Constraints:

- Works less well in distributed development efforts where teams are not located together
- Acceptance: forcing an Agile process on a development team that is unfamiliar with the approach

- Exceptions: mission-critical systems where failure is not an option at any cost (e.g. software for surgical procedures)

6 RELEVANT WEBSITE

www.agilemanifesto.org

Agile for responsive organizations – A Pocket Guide
Language: English

ISBN 9789401801829

Agile Foundation Courseware – English
Language: English

ISBN 9789401806893

Agile Foundation Exam – English
Languages: English, Dutch

Product code 103003180420B (EN)

Half Double

1 TITLE/ CURRENT VERSION

Half Double Methodology

2 THE BASICS

The Half Double methodology provides a comprehensive set of knowledge, concepts, techniques, and skills for the project manager who wants to create more impact of his projects in half the time.

3 SUMMARY

Whatever project your organization is launching – the rolling out of new products and services, improving customer experiences or business productivity – the Half Double Methodology can help.

Time after time, research reveals that only 36% of projects are successful. Most projects simply do not result in the impact they intended to. The Half Double Institute is a non-profit foundation whose methodology addresses this problem. Working in conjunction with three universities and 2,500 of the best project managers in Denmark, their methodology was created after comprehensively research. Trials of this methodology across 16 pilot projects in 16 different organizations, resulted in 87% of these pilot projects fulfilling or partly fulfilling the project success criteria. Not just delivered in time but even more important delivered with a business outcome such as increased revenue, reduced cost or reduced time to market. A vast improvement in project success.

Half Double focuses on three core principles – Impact, Flow, and Leadership – which leads to greater value creation and a proven increase in project success rates:

- Impact is all about navigating the project towards a given value creation. Being firm on impact and flexible on the deliverables. Not the other way around.
- Flow is about making sure the project has a weekly progression – giving us the opportunity to speed up the project and motivate people in the project.
- Leadership is about embracing the uncertainty inbound in all projects while making sure all stakeholders are onboard in a collaborative effort. Strong leadership will increase stakeholder satisfaction.

Half Double Foundation Guide and Handbook will inspire with simple tools and practices for readers to use in their organizations, enabling their projects to gain more impact in less time.

Look at Half Double's video case studies and find out how they have helped launch better products and services quicker and executed change faster. See how Half Double projects can be completed in less time, and result in double the impact.

4 TARGET AUDIENCE

Although the publication typically targets (senior) project managers, the processes described involve all roles with an interest in project management, such as senior executives, program and project managers, project team members, members of a project office, consultants and other specialists.

5 SCOPE AND CONSTRAINTS

The Half Double Methodology is a generic, hybrid approach that can be applied to any project.

Strengths

- Proven by researchers
- Extensive participation by different industry sectors and organizations and tested in real business projects
- Methodology is co-created by the most successful project managers and their best practise
- Generic and adaptive; it can be applied to any project
- A hybrid project management approach – thus able to co-exist and fit into other project management standards, both agile and traditional
- Certification programs (Foundation, Practitioner and Master) available through multiple partners and examination through APMG International

Constraints

- The Half Double Foundation Guide does not provide real life case examples describing the use of tools and templates – this can instead be found in the Handbook.

6 RELEVANT WEBSITES

www.halfdoubleinstitute.org/
https://apmg-international.com/product/half-double-certification

Half Double Methodology Handbook
Language: English
ISBN 9789401808323

ICB®

1 TITLE/ CURRENT VERSION

ICB4® – IPMA Individual Competence Baseline, Version 4

2 THE BASICS

The IPMA Individual Competence Baseline (ICB4) is the global standard for individual competences in project, programme and portfolio management.

3 SUMMARY

The International Project Management Association (IPMA) is a leading worldwide not-for-profit project management association with more than 60 member associations. IPMA published the first official version of the ICB (Version 2.0) in 1999, with a small modification in 2001. Version 3 was published in 2007 and Version 4 in 2015.

A central concept of the ICB4 is the 'eye of competence', which represents the three management domains of project, programme, and portfolio management. Based on a generic model each individual has to have perspective competences that address the context of his or her project, programme or portfolio, people competences that address personal and social topics and practices competences that address the specific technical aspects for managing his or her project, programme or portfolio.

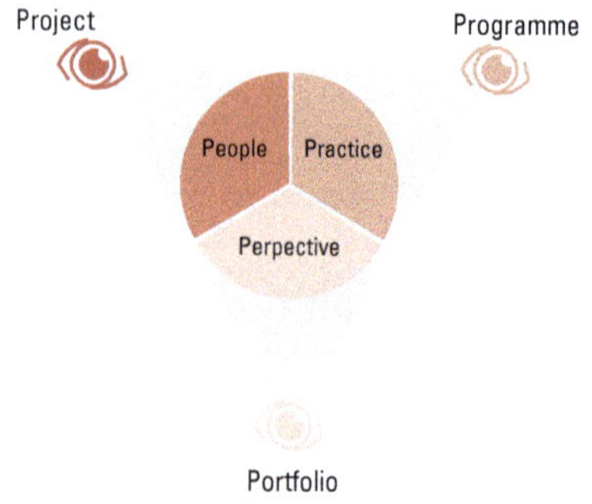

The ICB4 defines 29 competence elements:

- 5 Perspective competence elements
- 10 People competence elements
- 14 Practice competence elements.

Each competence element consists of a definition, the purpose, a description of the content, knowledge areas, skills and a list of related competence elements as well as a set of key competence indicators with a description and measures.

IPMA offers a four-level certification programme based on the IPMA Individual Competence Baseline (ICB4): IPMA level A-D.

4 TARGET AUDIENCE

The target audience consists of project, programme and portfolio managers and staff as well as general managers, assessors, coaches, HR managers and trainers involved in project, programme and portfolio management. This list is by no means exhaustive.

5 SCOPE AND CONSTRAINTS

The strength of the IPMA competence baseline is that it is a comprehensive inventory of competences an individual needs to have or to develop to successfully realise projects, programmes or portfolios. None of the other frameworks or methods for project, programme or portfolio management does this. The ICB4 framework is therefore most suitable as a reference model for the development and assessment of individual project, programme and portfolio managers. Further the ICB4 is applicable for all sectors and industries.

The ICB4 does not recommend or include specific methods or tools. Methods and tools may be defined by the organization. The project, programme or portfolio manager should choose appropriate methods and tools fit for the actual circumstances.

6 RELEVANT WEBSITE

Official IPMA website: www.ipma.world

Project Management by ICB4

Language: English

ISBN 9789401810920

Preparation Guide for IPMA Individual Certification

Language: English

ISBN 9789401812429

Courseware for IPMA Individual Certification based on Project Management by ICB4

ISBN 9789401812450

Online exam preparation for IPMA individual certification

ISBN: 10046VHEL9165

Kanban

1 TITLE/ CURRENT VERSION

Kanban

2 THE BASICS

Kanban provides a way for knowledge work teams to manage their work through visualization, managing the flow of work and continuous improvement. Heavily influenced by Lean, Kanban practices and principles are a great addition for agile teams and organizations to better manage how value is delivered to the customer.

3 SUMMARY

Kanban is a set of practices that help to bring structure to teams. This helps to organize the chaos that surrounds them by making the need for prioritization and focus clear. It is a way to uncover and identify problems in the work process so teams may solve them in order to deliver faster, more frequent and more predictable. Kanban is a way to put Lean thinking in practice. By making the work process transparent and actively managing the number of work items that are being worked on. The Kanban practices are:

- **Visualize** everything that is relevant to understand how workflows: our process, the work items, metrics and agreements around how we collaborate. Transparency helps create a shared understanding and focus discussions on which problems to solve. Kanban boards visualize how workflows through the team.
- **Manage the flow of work.** Not all work can be planned ahead. Small disruptions can lead to large delays. By managing bottlenecks, reducing wait time and active

focusing on what's most important we can deliver predictably. Through this practice teams gain insights into what work is most important, how to deliver it quickly and on promise, without having to sacrifice flexibility of priorities.

- **Limit Work in Progress.** Just by reducing the amount of task switching done in a team, a 60% faster time to market can be achieved. By limiting the number of items that are worked on at the same time we achieve important benefits. Instead of work being pushed into the team, new work is 'pulled' when there is capacity. Only when there is capacity, new work is started. This reduces queues, over burdening of the team and wait time. Kanban teams often use the phrase 'stop starting, start finishing' as their mantra.
- **Make process policies explicit.** Having transparency around the processes, agreements and prioritization mechanisms helps create clarity.
- **Improve collaboratively.** By taking a view of the work and improving with the people who are in the value chain we reduce suboptimization of the team.

Teams benefit from Kanban by enriching their current (delivery) practices with Kanban practices. The current way of working is always the starting point for adopting Kanban. This guarantees an easy to adopt and pragmatic way to evolve the value delivery process for teams and, eventually, organizations.

4 TARGET AUDIENCE

Kanban can bring significant benefits when one or more of the following statements are true:

- The team has more work than time (overloaded)
- It is not always clear who is working on what
- The team always receives feedback late or unpredictably

- Need for more cooperation and knowledge sharing (many islands with a lot of knowledge)
- A lot is being worked on, but little is actually achieved by constantly changing priorities
- It is unclear which activities contribute to the organizational goals
- Poorly planned, highly urgent work
- Multiple projects with many stakeholders go through the same team

Parts of the organization that typically implement Kanban practices:

- IT teams do more than just new product development
- Marketing, HR, Business Operations, Finance, Control, Legal, Sales
- DevOps, IT Operation teams
- Security, Architecture and BI teams (high level of expert knowledge)

5 SCOPE

Kanban has its foundation in Lean and has been enriched with agile practices. Although it was primarily used in IT operations (such as DevOps environments) in early stages of the method it has now grown to be applied in many areas of organizations such as marketing, HR, legal and sales. At the team level as well as program and portfolio levels of the organization.

6 RELEVANT WEBSITE

www.vhls.global/van-haren-certification/praqmatic-kanban-foundation/

Pragmatic Kanban Foundation Courseware – English

Language: English

ISBN 9789401805421

Kanban Foundation (eLearning)

Language: English

Product code 10022VHEL1111

Pragmatic Kanban Foundation – Exam

Language: English

Product code 106006180721B

P3.express

1 TITLE/ CURRENT VERSION

P3.express 2nd edition

2 THE BASICS

P3.express is a minimalist project management system that is easy to learn, easy to use, and easy to teach. P3.express is a response to the fact that project management systems are so complicated for typical use that most projects can't benefit from them and end up with intuitive, ad hoc approaches, which are risky and expensive.

This modern, practical method is provided with an open (non-proprietary) license and sponsored by the European Union.

3 SUMMARY

P3.express uses a cyclical system to make the activities simpler and more regular. There are monthly, weekly, and daily cycles, each of which focused on one aspect of managerial activities.

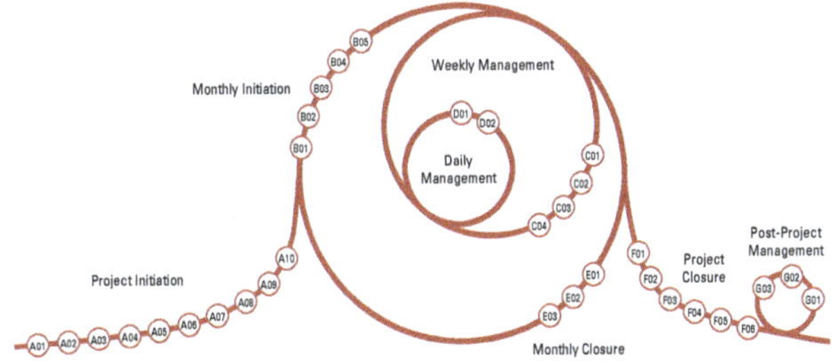

In addition to the said cycles, a project initiation activity group runs at the beginning and a project closure group at the end.

Finally, there's a post-project management group: a cycle run after the project is finished, to evaluate the benefits.

Four management documents are used in this process:

- Project Description: It contains basic information, such as purpose, requirements, and stakeholder list.
- Deliverables Map: It's a breakdown of the deliverables, usually as a mind map.
- Follow-Up Register: It's a list of all items that need follow-ups, such as issues and risks.
- Health Register: It contains the results of periodic project management peer-reviews and stakeholder satisfaction evaluations.

P3.express complies with the Nearly Universal Principles of Projects (NUPP).

The P3.express manual is available for free and in multiple languages:
https://p3.express/manual/v2/
In addition to the manual, there's a free interactive project simulation that teaches how a P3.express project works
https://p3.express/training/artophile-center/

4 TARGET AUDIENCE

P3.express is for everyone involved in leading projects, especially project managers.

5 SCOPE AND CONSTRAINTS

P3.express is designed for typical projects that most people are involved with and doesn't try to cover every possible project because that makes the system too complicated.

Moreover, it doesn't target 100% of the potential benefits of a structured project management method, but instead aims to cover 80% of those benefits with 20% of the effort.

P3.express is carefully designed to be compatible with both the adaptive (Agile) and predictive delivery methods.

6 RELEVANT WEBSITE

https://p3.express

P3.express Practitioner, project management certification

Language: English

Product code VHLSP3EXPPRAE

PM²

1 TITLE/ CURRENT VERSION

PM² Project Management Methodology, Version 3.01

2 THE BASICS

PM² is a project management methodology developed by the European Commission. Its purpose is to enable project managers to deliver solutions and benefits to their organizations by effectively managing the entire lifecycle of their projects.

PM² is the umbrella under which we find the European Commission's methodologies for managing (agile) projects, programmes and portfolios.

Currently the following elements are publicly available for PM²:

- For Project Management: *The PM² project management methodology Guide*, version 3.01
- For Agile: *The PM² – Agile guide*, version 3.01
- For Programme Management: *The PM² programme management Guide*, version 1.00
- For Portfolio Management: currently under review

The core is a strong but lightweight methodology for managing projects suited for medium to large projects in the public domain. Initially developed for internal projects with the European Commission but over time PM² has developed in a mature approach that is currently used by most European Agencies and Institutions within the European Union and increasingly by other national public service organizations across Europe. One of the distinguishing traits of PM² is the

emphasis on not only the process side but also the necessary mindset for successful project management.

3 SUMMARY

The current PM² project management methodology version 3.01 was launched in March 2021. It defines a clear and bespoke governance structure, has a phased approach and a very valuable and helpful set of supporting document templates for running projects. In its basis PM² is 'founded' on established best practice approaches to project management but other than most also addresses the challenge of not only delivering project results but also the benefits.

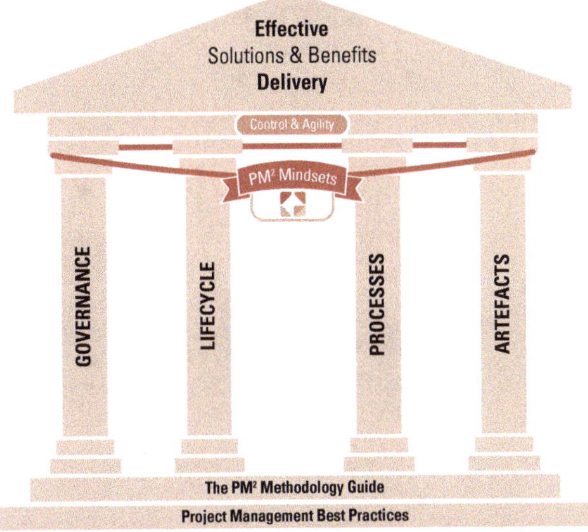

A certification in PM² is also provided in five different languages.

4 TARGET AUDIENCE

PM² is relevant for all functions on either the business or the solution side of projects, programmes and portfolios, such as senior managers, project owners, business and project managers, project team members and supporting staff.

5 SCOPE AND CONSTRAINTS

PM² is relevant for all organizations running projects in a public sector environment and for organizations and professionals (wanting to be) supplying services to agencies or institutions that have adopted PM².

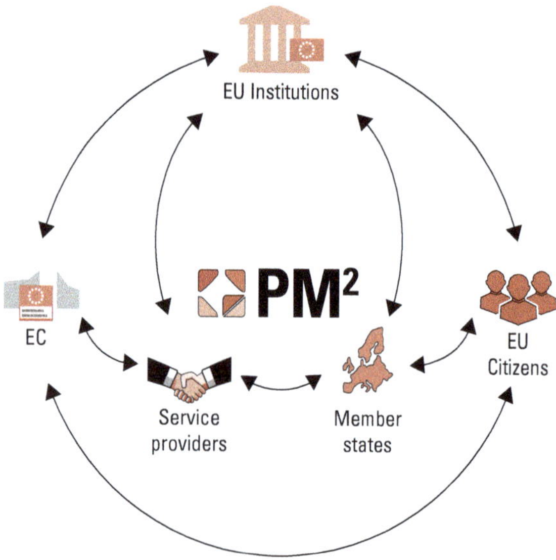

Strengths

- PM² has a very pragmatic and flexible approach to running projects
- Supports both traditional and more Agile approaches to projects
- Aligned with a broad range of existing PM Best Practices as well as IPMA's competence base line for Project Managers
- Has focus on both the outputs and the benefits of projects
- Highlights not only the procedural side of project management but also addresses the required mind-set for being truly successful in achieving results
- Tailored to suite projects in the public domain
- Strong 'installed base' in European Institutions
- Supported by a wealth of practical templates
- Offers an integrated approach to projects, programmes and portfolios

Constrains

- PM² as project management methodologies is aimed at mid to large size projects
- The focus is typically on projects with a clear business case for change

6 RELEVANT READING

The landing page of the European Union for PM²:
https://op.europa.eu/en/home

Certified PM² Foundation by PM² GROUP Courseware

Languages: English. French, Spanish, German, Italian

ISBN 9789401809016 (EN)

Certified PM² Foundation 3.1 by PM² GROUP – exam

Languages: English, Italian, French, Spanish, German

Product code PM2GROUPFCERF (EN)

PMBOK® Guide

1 TITLE/ CURRENT VERSION

A Guide to the Project Management Body of Knowledge (*PMBOK® Guide*) 7th Edition

2 THE BASICS

A Guide to the Project Management Body of Knowledge (PMBOK® Guide) is a guide providing a comprehensive set of knowledge, concepts, techniques and skills for the project management profession.

3 SUMMARY

The *PMBOK® Guide* is a publication from the Project Management Institute (PMI), an entity that is globally recognized as governing the project management discipline. The PMI was founded in 1969 in the US and has become one of the principal professional non-profit organizations in the specialism. The first edition of the guide was published in 1996; the latest English-language *PMBOK® Guide* – 7th Edition, was released in August 2021.

Whereas the *PMBOK® Guide* 6th edition is process-based, the 7th edition is principle-based. As a result, the 756 pages of the *PMBOK® Guide* 6th edition has been slimmed down to 274 pages for the 7th edition. The 6th edition is grounded in technical processes, inputs, tools and techniques, and outputs for the project manager, the *PMBOK® Guide* 7th edition is driven by skills and resources for the team to deliver value-based outcomes. The most significant difference between the *PMBOK® Guide* 7th and 6th editions is the shift of focus from very technically driven processes and tools to more over-arching principles anyone involved with project management work can use to be successful. This approach is consistent with other management standards such as ISO 21500 for Project management, ISO/IEC 9001:2008 the international norm for quality standards, and the Software Engineering Institute's CMMI.

In short, the *PMBOK® Guide* 6th edition was designed by the PMI to be project manager and process-focused, while the new 7th edition is project team and outcome-focused. As a result, the five process groups have been replaced by twelve Project Delivery Principles: Stewardship, Team, Stakeholders, Value, Holistic Thinking, Quality, Complexity, Leadership, Tailoring, Opportunities & Threats, Adaptability & Resilience, Change management.

The ten knowledge areas of the *PMBOK® Guide* 6th edition have been replaced by a set of eight performance domains in the *PMBOK® Guide* 7th edition. The PMI defines a domain as "groups of related activities that are critical for the effective delivery of project outcomes." These performance domains are: Team, Stakeholders, Life cycle, Planning, Navigating Uncertainty and Ambiguity, Delivery, Performance, Project Work.

4 TARGET AUDIENCE

Although the publication typically targets (senior) project managers, the principles described involve all roles with an interest in project management, such as senior executives, programme and project managers, project team members, members of a project office, customers and other stakeholders, consultants and other specialists. As an introduction, an easy accessible pocket publication is also available, aimed at a broader audience involved in projects.

5 SCOPE AND CONSTRAINTS

PMBOK® Guide is a generic approach that can be applied to any project.

Strengths

- Extensive participation by different industry sectors and organizations that are using project management all over the world
- Recognized as a 'world class' standard in the profession and, because of that, used as the book of reference for many other project management standards and methods
- Generic; it can be applied to any project
- Fully aligned to the latest global project management standard, ISO 21500
- Evolution and continuous improvement (every four years) in line with modern concepts of quality
- Certification programmes (PMP and CAPM) associated and guaranteed deployment of accreditation skills from all over the world.
- Fully aligned with the broader concept of project, programme and portfolio management (PMI provides additional standards for this)

Constraints

- It is essential that the *PMBOK® Guide's* pivot from a process focus to a value delivery focus is reflective of the global shift in project management itself.

6 RELEVANT WEBSITE

www.pmi.org/

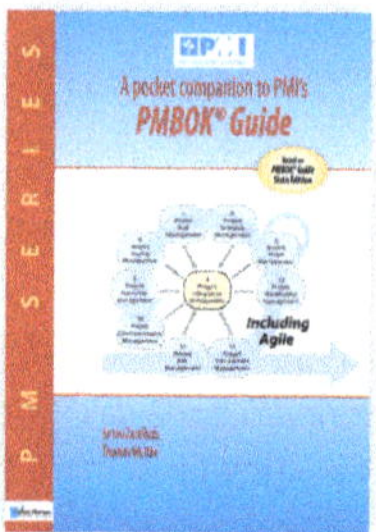

A Pocket Companion to PMI's PMBOK® Guide

Languages: English, Dutch

ISBN 9789401801102

PMO
(Project Management Office)

1 TITLE

Project Management Office (PMO

2 THE BASICS

A Project Management Office (PMO) is an organizational entity that operates independently or in collaboration with other PMOs, offering mandated services and non-mandated services with responsibilities relating to delivering and managing those services. Mandated services are PMO services that must be provided by one or more PMOs and are mandatory for the customer(s) to use, regardless of whether they choose to develop or utilize their capabilities. On the other hand, non-mandated services are optional services offered by the PMO based on specific organizational needs.

AIPMO, Association of International Project Management Officers, is a professional association representing International Project Management Officers (IPMO), including project, program, and portfolio managers.

There are hundreds of types of PMOs, making them difficult to categorize, especially as they evolve over time and may change type. Two common categories include:

1. Delivery and non-delivery PMOs
2. Initiative-specific and organizational PMOs

Delivery PMOs are delivery-focused PMOs that concentrate on project execution and delivery. They support project managers, provide project management tools and templates, and ensure projects are delivered successfully, meeting objectives within defined timelines and budgets. Non-delivery PMOs focus on governance, standards, methodologies, and strategic alignment rather than directly executing projects.

Initiative-specific PMOs are temporary entities established to support a specific initiative. In contrast, organizational PMOs are semi-permanent entities embedded in the organization to varying degrees, supporting two or more endeavors. These could include projects, programs, and portfolios.

For both categories, one state can evolve into the other state.

The term PMO has become a generic term for all types of PMOs—for example, the strategy management office, finance management office, program management office, and project management office are all types of Management Offices (MOs).

A PMO's responsibilities will depend on its mandate and what is needed to help ensure the project's success, either directly (as a delivery PMO) or indirectly as a non-delivery PMO. When formalized, these responsibilities are described as services and become part of the PMO's success criteria.

3 SUMMARY

As a PMO can offer hundreds of potential services, described in a PMO Service Catalog, the services are categorized under Service domains (as outlined in the *PMO Services and Capabilities* book by AIPMO).

Examples of services include developing project management standards, providing governance frameworks, offering tools and resources to streamline project execution, monitoring project progress, managing risks, ensuring effective resource allocation, and ensuring alignment with organizational goals and benefits realization.

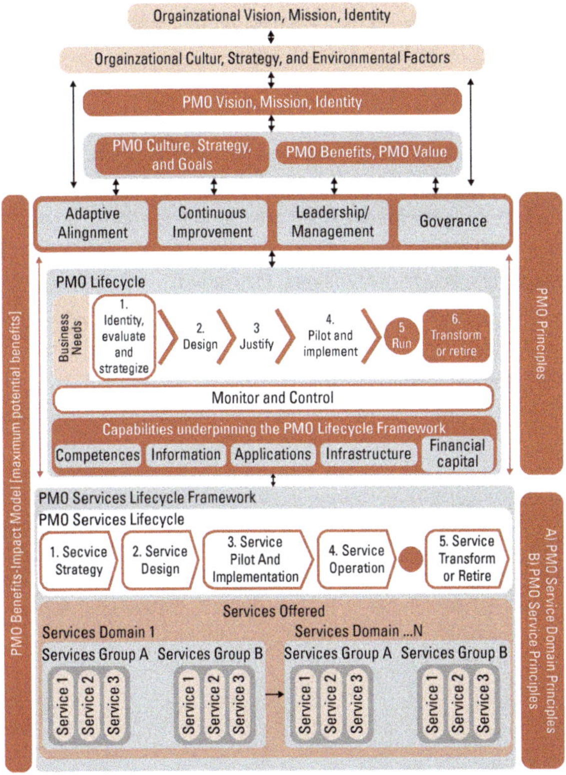

Orgainzational Vision, Mission, Identity
Orgainzational Cultur, Strategy, and Environmental Factors
PMO Vision, Mission, Identity
PMO Culture, Strategy, and Goals
PMO Benefits, PMO Value
Adaptive Alingnment
Continuous Improvement
Leadership/ Management
Goverance
PMO Lifecycle
Business Needs
1. Identity, evaluate and strategize
2. Design
3 Justify
4. Pilot and implement
5 Run
6. Transform or retire
Monitor and Control
Capabilities underpinning the PMO Lifecycle Framework
Competences
Information
Applications
Infrastructure
Financial capital
PMO Services Lifecycle Framework
PMO Services Lifecycle
1. Secvice Strategy
2. Service Design
3. Service Pilot And Implementation
4. Service Operation
5. Service Transform or Retire
Services Offered
Services Domain 1
Services Group A
Services Group B
Services Domain ...N
Services Group A
Services Group B
Service 1
Service 2
Service 3
Service 1
Service 2
Service 3
Service 1
Service 2
Service 3
Service 1
Service 2
Service 3
PMO Benefits-Impact Model [maximum potential benefits]
PMO Principles
A) PMO Service Domain Principles
B) PMO Service Principles

PMOs exist throughout an organization and may not even use the term PMO in its name.

Identifying the need for one or more PMOs, designing, implementing, operating, optimizing, and retiring them or parts of their services is complex. Therefore, it is important to use a robust framework and methodology to reduce the risks of failure.*PMO Strategic Lifecycle Framework (Source AIPMO)*

4 TARGET AUDIENCE

The PMO is designed for organizations that manage diverse projects, from small-scale initiatives to large transformational programs. The target audience for a PMO includes:

- Project Portfolio Managers, Project Managers, PMO Managers/Directors, Business Analysts, IT Managers, Change Managers, Program Managers, Executives

5 RELEVANT WEBSITE

https://www.aipmo.org/

PRINCE2®

1 TITLE/ CURRENT VERSION

PRINCE2® 7th edition (PRojects IN Controlled Enviroments). First released in 1989 and regularly revised, in 1996, 2005, 2017 and recently in 2023. Since 2021, PRINCE2 is owned by PeopleCert Ltd.

2 THE BASICS

PRINCE2 is still one of the most widely used methods for managing projects in the world. It is a structured and process-based project management method. Since it is a best practice method, the 7th edition responds to a number of changes that have taken place in the world and in the profession of project management since the previous edition was launched.

3 SUMMARY

PRINCE2 is for all, meaning it has been designed to be generic and can be applied to any project regardless of project type, scale, (profit/non-profit) organization, geography or culture.

The digital revolution, the speed of change, the rise of Agile ways of working and the increased volatility and uncertainty in the world means that project management *must* evolve to meet these demands.

When updating a method, the tendency can be simply adding new material to the existing content, resulting in more rather than better guidance. Instead, the decision was taken to go back to the basics and challenge every aspect of PRINCE2 to ensure that its inclusion was required and contributed to the method being fit for now and many years to come.

The overall structure offers elements of project management surrounding people from its mids. principles, practices (previously called Themes) and a set of processes that make up the lifecycle of a project in its context. These five integrated elements are:

People – projects need people, mainly those working on the project and those affected by it. An understanding of needs, capabilities and motivations of the people involved and the relationships between them is crucial for project success. People is the centre of the method.
Principles – PRINCE2 is a principle-centered method that provides guidance every PRINCE2 project should adhere to. There are seven principles: ensure continued Business Justfication, learn from experience, define roles, responsibilities and relationships, manage by stages, manage by exception, focus on products, tailor to suit the project.
Practices – give guidance on how to apply and tailor PRINCE2. Each practice follows a common format to enable effective use. There are seven practices: Business Case, Organizing, Plans, Quality, Risk, Issues and Progress.
Processes – the process model explains the 'PRINCE2 journey' through any project. It gives guidance to their purpose, objective, context, activities and application of the Practices within that process.
Project Context – the principles, practices and process are applied by the people involved to ensure that the method is fit for the project context.

The PRINCE2 management products are documented in an Appendix with guidance on how they could be tailored.

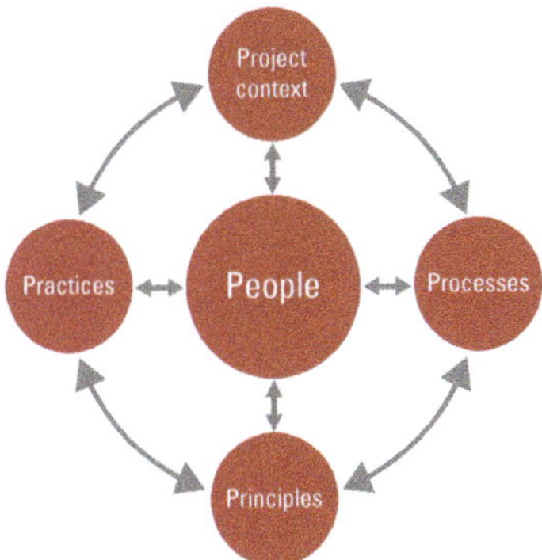

4 TARGET AUDIENCE

Project managers, project team members, senior management responsible for decision-making in projects.

5 SCOPE AND CONSTRAINTS

PRINCE2 is generic and is suitable for a wide range of organizations and environments. It provides a 'common and universal language' regardless of project scale, type, organization, geography or culture.

Contraints: PRINCE2 is not intended to cover every aspect of project management.

Specialist aspect of project work: the strength of PRINCE2 is its flexibility and that it is not specific to particular industries or delivery and engineering practices.

Detailed project management techniques: the method highlights various techniques that support the practices but are not documented in detail. Examples are: release planning, Kanban, critical path analysis and earned value management.

6 RELEVANT WEBSITE

www.axelos.com

Projectmanagement op basis van PRINCE2 7 Foundation courseware

Language: Dutch

ISBN 9789401811613

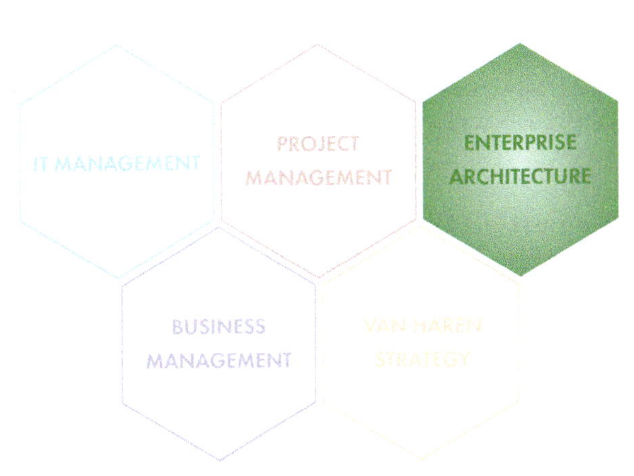
IT MANAGEMENT
PROJECT MANAGEMENT
ENTERPRISE ARCHITECTURE
BUSINESS MANAGEMENT
VAN HAREN STRATEGY

ArchiMate®

1 TITLE/ CURRENT VERSION

The ArchiMate® 3.2 Specification, a standard of The Open Group

2 THE BASICS

The ArchiMate Specification defines an open and independent modeling language for Enterprise Architecture that is supported by different tool vendors and consulting firms. The ArchiMate language enables enterprise architects to describe, analyse, and visualize the relationships between business domains in an unambiguous way.

3 SUMMARY

Developed by the members of The Open Group, the ArchiMate® 3.2 Specification was released in October 2022 and is aligned with the TOGAF® Standard, the world's most popular Enterprise Architecture framework. As a result, enterprise architects using the language can improve the way key business and IT stakeholders collaborate and adapt to change.

The standard contains the formal definition of the ArchiMate notation as a visual design language, together with concepts for specifying interrelated architectures, and specific viewpoints for typical stakeholders. The standard also includes a chapter addressing considerations regarding language extensions.

The contents of the standard include the following:

- The introduction, including the objectives, overview, conformance requirements, and terminology
- Definitions of the general terms used in the specification
- The structure of the modeling language

- The generic metamodel of the language
- The relationships in the language
- A detailed breakdown of the modeling framework covering the motivation elements, strategy layer elements, and the three core layers (Business/Application/Technology)
- Relationships between core layers
- Implementation and migration layer elements
- The concepts of stakeholders, architecture viewpoints, and views, as well as the ArchiMate viewpoint mechanism
- Mechanisms for customizing the language
- Notation overviews and summaries

The ArchiMate modeling language improves collaboration by enabling clearer understanding across multiple functions, including business executives, enterprise architects, systems analysts, software engineers, business process consultants, and infrastructure engineers. The standard enables the creation of fully integrated models of an organization's Enterprise Architecture, the motivation behind it, and the programs, projects, and migration paths to implement it. The language uses the terminology defined in the TOGAF framework and supports modeling throughout the TOGAF Architecture Development Method (ADM) cycle.

4 TARGET AUDIENCE

Enterprise architects, business architects, IT architects, application architects, data architects, software architects, systems architects, solutions architects, infrastructure architects, process architects, domain architects, product managers, operational managers, senior managers, project leaders, and anyone committed to working within the reference framework defined by an Enterprise Architecture.

5 SCOPE

The role of the ArchiMate standard is to provide a graphical language for the representation of Enterprise Architectures over time (i.e., including transformation and migration planning), as well as their motivation and rationale. The ArchiMate modeling language provides a uniform representation for diagrams that describe Enterprise Architectures, and offers an integrated approach to describe and visualize the different architecture domains, together with their underlying relations and dependencies.

The design of the ArchiMate language started from a set of relatively generic concepts (objects and relations), which have been specialized for application at the different architectural layers for an Enterprise Architecture. The most important design restriction on the language is that it has been explicitly designed to be as compact as possible, yet still usable for most Enterprise Architecture modeling tasks. In the interest of simplicity of learning and use, the ArchiMate language has been limited to the concepts that suffice for modeling the proverbial 80% of practical cases.

6 RELEVANT WEBSITE

www.opengroup.org/archimate

ArchiMate® 3.2 Specification

Language: English

ISBN 9789401809559 (EN)

BIAN®

1 TITLE/ CURRENT VERSION

BIAN® 2nd Edition – A framework for the financial services industry

2 THE BASICS

The Banking Industry Architecture Network (BIAN) is an association of banks, solution providers and educational institutions with the shared aim of defining a semantic service operation standard for the banking industry. BIAN's expectation is that a standard definition of the business functions, service interactions and information that describe the general workings of any bank or organization in the banking ecosystem, will be a significant benefit to the industry. When compared to a proliferation of proprietary designs, such an industry standard provides the following main benefits:

- it enables the more efficient and effective development and integration of software solutions for the Banking Industry
- it improves the operational efficiency within the industry and provides the opportunity for greater solution and capability re-use within and among organizations in the Banking Industry
- it supports the current need for more industry integration and collaboration by the usage of (open) API's
- it supports the adoption of more flexible business service sourcing models and enhances the evolution and adoption of shared 3rd party business services.

3 SUMMARY

At the core of BIAN's proposition is the adoption of a capability-oriented approach to architecting the systems that support the

Banking Industry. This approach is fundamentally different from the prevailing 'process–centric' designs.

BIAN's Reference Architecture for the Financial Industry is developed by the BIAN members, Its development is iterative, relying on the active contribution of industry participants to build consensus and encourage adoption. BIAN coordinates the evolution of the BIAN Architecture on behalf of its membership with regular version releases to the industry and seeks feedback to help continually expand and refine its content. The main BIAN documents deliverables include:

BIAN's Reference Architecture for the Financial Services Industry:

- The BIAN Metamodel
- The high -level BIAN reference map: the BIAN Service Landscape
- The BIAN Service Domain and Service Operations-definitions: a Mutually Exclusive Commonly Exhaustive (MECE) collection of service centers and their services, as building blocks for a bank's functionality and service exchanges
- The BIAN Information Architecture, a model providing the MECE collection of Business Objects, supporting the information needs of a bank
- The BIAN Semantic API definitions, describing the Service Operations in more detail
- The BIAN Business Scenario definitions, examples of usage of the BIAN building blocks

The BIAN Business Capability definitions. Support in applying BIAN:

- The BIAN How-to Guide series, a collection of documents targeting different audiences
- BIAN webinars, containing real-life examples of use;
- The BIAN book: BIAN 2nd edition – A framework for the financial services industry
- Training and certification

The BIAN Architecture is published in an UML repository for its Members and an HTML read-only version which is freely available on the BIAN website (https://bian.org/).

Relating BIAN to TOGAF

By looking at BIAN as a pool of industry-specific architecture deliverables and at TOGAF as the overall framework for architecture work, it's easy to understand the synergy between the BIAN deliverables and the TOGAF framework.

BIAN provides content in a specific structure. When applying TOGAF in a banking environment, BIAN content speeds up the work and improves quality. On the other hand, TOGAF facilitates architecture development work by providing a structured approach and a complete structure of relevant artifacts, thus adding value to the BIAN deliverables.

4 TARGET AUDIENCE

Enterprise architects, business architects, IT architects, application architects, data architects, system architects, solutions architects, process architects, domain architects, senior managers, project leaders and anyone committed to work within the frame of reference designed by an Enterprise Architecture.

5 SCOPE

The role of the BIAN Architecture is to provide a common language for the definition of a banking ecosystem. This language is canonical and implementation- and technology agnostic, so it could be applied in a wide range of organizations and technology environments.

By combining the different layers of the overall BIAN Architecture, it provides financial institutions all around the globe a unique starting point for business and IT renewal in a very controlled and consistent manner.

Today BIAN is primarily focusing on the Banking industry. But other financial services, like Insurance and Pensions can already benefit from it. It is expected that that BIAN will deliver models for these industries in the upcoming years.

6 RELEVANT WEBSITE

https://bian.org/

BIAN 2nd Edition – A framework for the financial services industry

Language: English

ISBN 9789401807685

BIAN Banking Architecture Foundation Courseware

Languages: English, Spanish

ISBN 9789401807906 (EN)

BIAN Banking Architecture Foundation Certification

Language: English, Spanish

Product code VHLSBIANBIANB (EN)

IT4IT™

1 TITLE/ CURRENT VERSION

The IT4IT™ Standard, Version 3.0, a standard of The Open Group

2 THE BASICS

The Open Group IT4IT Standard describes a reference architecture that can be used to manage the business of Information Technology (IT) and the associated end-to-end lifecycle management of Digital Products.

3 SUMMARY

At the most basic level, the IT4IT Standard defines the "Digital Management" of "Digital Products" in order to create an efficient value delivery. The IT4IT Standard is about defining the value stream, the associated functions, and the data objects needed to control the planning, development, delivery, and run management of Digital Products.

The IT4IT Standard:

- Is intended to provide a prescriptive Target Architecture and clear guidance for the transformation of existing technology

management practices for a faster, scalable, automated, and practical approach to deploying product-based investment models and providing an unprecedented level of operational control and measurable value
- Is independent of specific technologies, vendors, organization structures, process models, and methodologies
- Can be mapped to any existing technology landscape, and is flexible enough to accommodate the continuing evolution of operational and management paradigms for technology
- Addresses a critical gap in the Digital Transformation toolkit: the need for a unifying architectural model that describes and connects the capabilities, value streams, functions, and operational data needed to manage a Digital Product Portfolio at scale

4 TARGET AUDIENCE

The target audience for the standard consists of:
- C-level executives responsible for Digital Transformation, as a top-down view of digital value creation
- Product Managers and Product Marketing Managers whose portfolios include significant digital content, as a way to integrate marketing priorities with product delivery practices
- Governance, risk, and compliance practitioners, as a guide to controlling a modern digital landscape
- Enterprise and IT Architects, as a template for IT tool rationalization and for governing end-to-end technology management architectures
- Technology buyers, as the basis for Requests for Information (RFIs) and Requests for Proposals (RFPs) and as a template for evaluating product completeness
- Consultants and assessors, as a guide for evaluating current practice against a well-defined standard

- Technology vendors, as a guide for product design and customer integrations
- Technical support staff, as a guide for automating and scaling up support services to deal with modern technology deployment velocity

5 SCOPE

The IT4IT Standard addresses a critical gap in the Digital Transformation toolkit: the need for a unifying architectural model that describes and connects the capabilities, value streams, functions, and operational data needed to manage a Digital Product Portfolio at scale.

Traditional management paradigms, in which the technology budget is a combination of one-off projects and keep-the-lights-on operations, have constrained the value that could be delivered by technology. A fundamentally different approach is needed.

In recent years, this need continues to evolve rapidly as business management itself has become digital management. In other words, as the business delivers Digital Products, IT becomes the business.

By showing how to shift the focus of digital investment from project expense to product-based value delivery, the IT4IT Standard provides a powerful model for standardizing the digital automation fabric to support constant innovation and accelerated digital service delivery.

6 RELEVANT WEBSITE

www.opengroup.org/IT4IT

The IT4IT™ Standard, Version 3.0

Language: English

ISBN 9789401809405

Open Agile Architecture™

1 TITLE/ CURRENT VERSION

The Open Agile Architecture™ Standard, a standard of The Open Group

2 THE BASICS

The Open Agile Architecture Standard covers Digital Transformation of the enterprise, together with Agile Transformation of the enterprise.

3 SUMMARY

The Open Agile Architecture Standard (also known as the O-AA™ Standard) is an approach to architecture at scale with agility that takes an outcome-based, customer-focused, and product-centered approach to guide business and technology leaders through a Digital Transformation using an Agile approach.

The digital enterprise is shaped by people who work in the context of an enterprise's organization and culture that needs to evolve toward agility at scale. Agile teams drive the enterprise's Digital Transformation by inventing new business models, delivering superior customer experience, developing digital products, and architecting highly-automated operating systems.

The O-AA Standard was consciously designed keeping the needs of all business stakeholders in mind:

- **Business Leaders** – to drive the enterprise's Digital and Agile change journey
- **Enterprise Architects** – to extend their scope of influence in an Agile at scale world

- **Product Managers** – to help transform customer experience, innovate products, and generate growth
- **Product Owners** – to accelerate their transformation from managing feature backlog to steering value delivery
- **Operations Managers** – to enable them to leverage lean and automation to generate sustainable competitive advantages
- **Software Engineers** – to leverage the power of digital technologies to co-innovate with the business

The more Agile the enterprise, the faster the learning cycles, and faster learning cycles translate to shorter time-to-market resulting in more agility. By adopting the O-AA Standard, your organization can capitalize on this accelerated learning cycle, meaning your Agile and Digital capabilities continuously and simultaneously co-create one another.

Outcome-Based, Product-Centric, Team-Led

Product-centricity refers to the shift from temporary organizational structures – projects – to permanent ones. A product-centric organization is composed of cross-functional teams which are responsible for developing products or services and operating or running them, with each member bringing expertise from their own domain:

- Executives are looking for innovative business models that generate profitable revenue growth
- Technology Leaders bring flexible and adaptive new software technologies and have popularized new Agile ways of working
- Operation Teams are leveraging capabilities provided by lean, automation, and software platforms to improve operational excellence

- Product Managers bring customer focus to the table along with new disciplines such as design thinking
- Compliance Officers need to ensure that privacy and security regulations remain applied throughout the organization

It also provides a framework and common language for your teams to function effectively to develop and deliver a collaborative, nimble operating model that enables success.

4 TARGET AUDIENCE

- Agilists who need to understand the importance of architecture when shifting toward an Agile at scale model, and who want to learn architecture skills
- Enterprise architects, solution architects, security architects, and software architects who want to stay relevant in an Agile at scale world and who need to learn new architecture skills for the digital age
- Business managers and executives who need to learn the importance of the architecture discipline, and who need to influence architecture decisions

5 SCOPE

The Open Agile Architecture Standard provides guidance and test practices for the transition to Agile and Digital contexts.

6 RELEVANT WEBSITE

www.opengroup.org/agilearchitecture

Open Agile Architecture™ – A Standard of The Open Group

Language: English

ISBN 9789401809405

TOGAF®

1 TITLE/ CURRENT VERSION

The TOGAF® Standard, 10th Edition, a standard of The Open Group

2 THE BASICS

The TOGAF® Standard is a proven Enterprise Architecture methodology and framework used by the world's leading organizations to improve business efficiency.

3 SUMMARY

The TOGAF® Standard is a proven Enterprise Architecture methodology and framework used by the world's leading organizations to improve business efficiency. It is the most prominent and reliable Enterprise Architecture standard, ensuring consistent standards, methods, and communication among Enterprise Architecture professionals. Enterprise Architecture professionals fluent in the TOGAF framework and method enjoy greater industry credibility, job effectiveness, and career opportunities. Use of the TOGAF Standard helps practitioners avoid being locked into proprietary methods, utilize resources more efficiently and effectively, and realize a greater return on investment.

The TOGAF Standard has been continuously evolved and improved by the members of The Open Group since it was first published by them in 1995. The Open Group is a global consortium that enables the achievement of business objectives through technology standards. With more than 870 member organizations, the diverse membership spans all sectors of the IT community — customers, systems and solutions suppliers,

tool vendors, integrators and consultants, as well as academics and researchers.

The TOGAF Standard, 10th Edition builds on previous versions of the TOGAF Standard, expanding and updating the material available to architecture practitioners to assist them in building a sustainable Enterprise Architecture.

The TOGAF documentation set is structured to address the transition from common universal concepts to the unique configuration within an organization. It includes the formal TOGAF Standard and a broader Body of Knowledge in the TOGAF Library, as shown below.

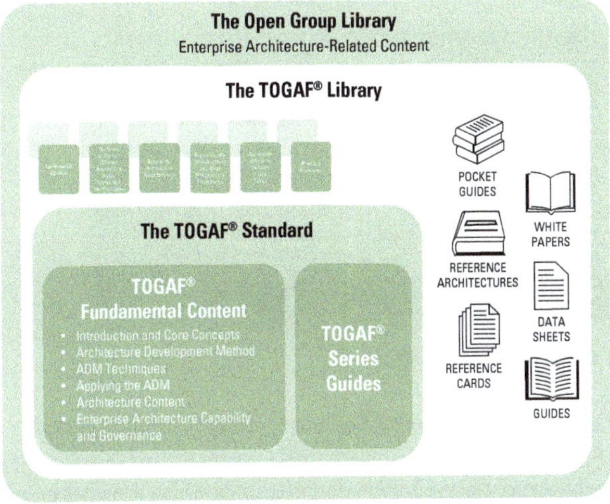

Figure 1: The TOGAF Documentation Set

The TOGAF Fundamental Content includes the universal concepts of Enterprise Architecture. The TOGAF Series Guides take these concepts and make them actionable. Together, the TOGAF Fundamental Content and the TOGAF Series Guides are the TOGAF Standard.

The intent of dividing the TOGAF Standard into these separate documents is to allow for different areas of specialization to be considered in detail and potentially addressed in isolation. Although all the constituent documents work together as a whole, it is also feasible to select particular documents for adoption while excluding others.

An Overview of the TOGAF Standard

Figure 2: The TOGAF Standard

The TOGAF Fundamental Content consists of six documents. Central to the TOGAF Fundamental Content is the TOGAF Architecture Development Method (ADM), which provides a tested and repeatable process for developing architectures. The TOGAF Series Guides consist of a series of best practice documents, which is expected to expand over time as the

professional Body of Knowledge that forms the TOGAF Standard expands with more stable best practice. The role of the TOGAF Series Guides is to build upon the content provided in the TOGAF Fundamental Content by providing extended guidance for specific topics, concerns, and use-cases.

4 TARGET AUDIENCE

Enterprise architects, business architects, IT architects, data architects, systems architects, solutions architects; architecture service providers and tools suppliers.

5 SCOPE

The TOGAF Standard can be used for developing a broad range of different Enterprise Architectures.

The TOGAF Standard complements, and can be used in conjunction with, other frameworks that are more focused on specific deliverables for particular vertical sectors such as Government, Telecommunications, Manufacturing, Defense, and Finance. The key to the TOGAF Standard is the method – the TOGAF Architecture Development Method (ADM) – for developing an Enterprise Architecture that addresses business needs.

6 RELEVANT WEBSITE

www.opengroup.org/togaf

Set of seven volumes; this is the official core book for the TOGAF standard 10th Edition

Language: English

ISBN TogafSet10th (EN)

TOGAF 10th Edition - A Pocket Guide

Language: English

ISBN 9789401808569

IT MANAGEMENT
PROJECT MANAGEMENT
ENTERPRISE ARCHITECTURE
BUSINESS MANAGEMENT
VAN HAREN STRATEGY

Balanced Scorecard

1 TITLE/ CURRENT VERSION

Balanced Scorecard

2 THE BASICS

The Balanced Scorecard is a strategic planning and management framework that is used to "align business activities to the vision and strategy of the organization, improve internal and external communications, and monitor organization performance against strategic goals" (source: Balanced Scorecard Institute).

3 SUMMARY

The Balanced Scorecard was first published in 1992 by Robert Kaplan (Harvard Business School) and David Norton as a performance measurement framework that added strategic non-financial performance measures to traditional financial metrics to give managers and executives a more 'balanced' view of organizational performance. The Balanced Scorecard has evolved from its early use as a simple performance measurement 'dashboard' to a full strategic planning and management system. It transforms an organization's strategic plan from a passive document into the 'marching orders' for the organization on a daily basis.

The Balanced Scorecard is a management system (not only a measurement system) that enables organizations to clarify their vision and strategy and translate these into action. It provides feedback around both the internal business processes and external outcomes in order to continuously improve strategic performance and results.

The Balanced Scorecard has four perspectives (see Figure):

1. The Learning and Growth Perspective: employee training and corporate cultural attitudes related to both individual and corporate self-improvement.
2. The Business Process Perspective: internal business processes.
3. The Customer Perspective: customer focus and customer satisfaction.
4. The Financial Perspective: financial and financial-related data, such as risk assessment and cost-benefit data.

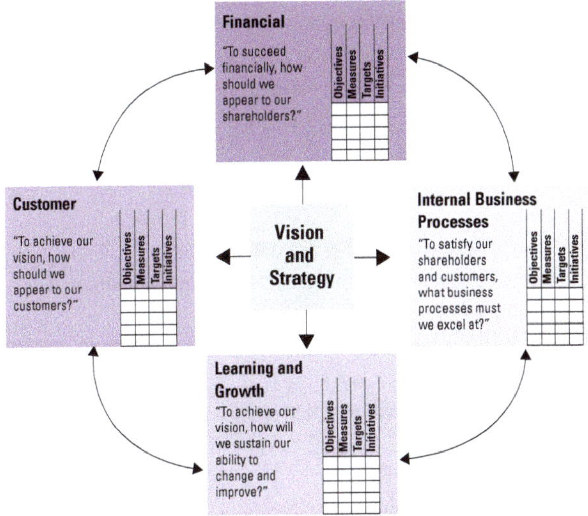

Figure: Four perspectives of the Balanced Scorecard

A Balanced Scorecard should be enhanced with cause-and-effect relationships between measures: outcome measures (lag indicators of past performance) and performance drivers (lead indicators). A well-developed scorecard should contain a good mix of these two metrics.

4 TARGET AUDIENCE

Senior management, strategic planners, business managers.

5 SCOPE AND CONSTRAINTS

The Balanced Scorecard was initially developed at an enterprise level. It can easily be adapted to align IT projects, IT departments and IT performance to the needs of the business.

- The Balanced Scorecard is used extensively in business and industry, government and non-profit organizations worldwide
- Use of an IT Balanced Scorecard is one of the most effective means to support the board and management in achieving IT and business alignment

Constraints

- Visions and strategies that are not actionable
- Strategies that are not linked to departmental, team and individual goals
- Strategies that are not linked to long- and short-term resource allocation
- Feedback that is tactical, not strategic

6 RELEVANT WEBSITE

www.balancedscorecard.org

BiSL®

1 TITLE/ CURRENT VERSION

BiSL® (Business Information Services Library) 4th Edition

2 THE BASICS

BiSL (Business Information Services Library) is a framework and collection of best practices for business information management.

3 SUMMARY

BiSL (Business Information Services Library) was developed by a Dutch IT service provider, PinkRoccade, and made public and transferred to the public domain in 2005. The current version is the 4th Edition, published in 2024.

BiSL focuses on how business organizations can improve control over their information provisioning: demand for business support, use of information systems and non-automized information provision and contracts and other arrangements with IT suppliers. BiSL offers guidance in business information management: support for the use of information provisioning in the business processes, operational IT control and information management.

The library consists of a framework, best practices, standard templates and a self-assessment. The BiSL framework gives a description of all the processes that enable the control of information provisioning from a business perspective (see Figure).

The framework distinguishes seven process clusters, which are positioned at the operational, managing and strategic levels (see Figure).

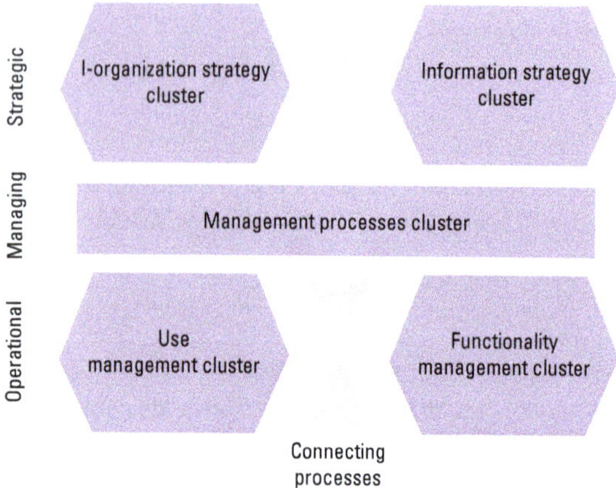

The *use management* cluster provides optimum, on-going support in use of the information provision. The *functionality management* cluster structures and effects changes in information provision. The *connecting processes* cluster focuses on decision-making related to which changes need to be made to the information provision, and how they are implemented within the user organization.

The *management processes* cluster ensures that all the activities within the business information management domain are managed in an integrated way.

The strategic processes clusters ensure that realizable strategic plans and policies are developed for the information provision as well as for the business information management organization.

4 TARGET AUDIENCE

BiSL is primarily aimed at business management, information management and professionals who wish to improve the support of their business processes by realizing a better automated and non-automated information provision. Of course, also students and training organizations in this field of interest belong to the target audience.

5 SCOPE AND CONSTRAINTS

The scope of BiSL is the support, usage, maintenance, renovation and policy of the information provision and the management and governance of all related activities.

Strengths

- It offers a stable framework and a common language for business information management.
- It fills the gap between the business and IT functions. BiSL recognizes and addresses management issues that are increasingly important.
- The application of BiSL in the Netherlands is widely spread amongst various types of organizations, thus a lot of experience with BiSL has been gained. Many of these experiences have been translated into applicable best practices, templates, etc, which are available on the internet.

- Internationally accredited exams are available.

Constraints

- Although the BiSL framework, books and best practices have been translated in different languages, the application of BiSL outside the Netherlands is still relatively limited

6 RELEVANT WEBSITE

www.vanharen.net

BiSL - Een framework voor business informatiemanagement 4de editie
Language: Dutch

ISBN 9789401811460

BiSL® 4de editie Foundation Courseware
Language: English, Dutch

ISBN 9789401812887 (EN)

BiSL 4th Edition Foundation Examination
Languages: English, Dutch

Product code 40023BISL4ENO (EN)

CATS CM®

1 TITLE/ CURRENT VERSION

CATS CM® version 4

2 THE BASICS

CATS CM® exists since 2005 and has evolved into the ultimate best practice contract management methodology. Thousands of professionals and organizations follow this standard. CATS stands for Contract Administration and Tracking Scenarios. In contract management, the focus is on achieving the intended contract objectives, which reflect everything an organization aims to achieve with the contract, aligning with its mission, vision, and legal regulations.

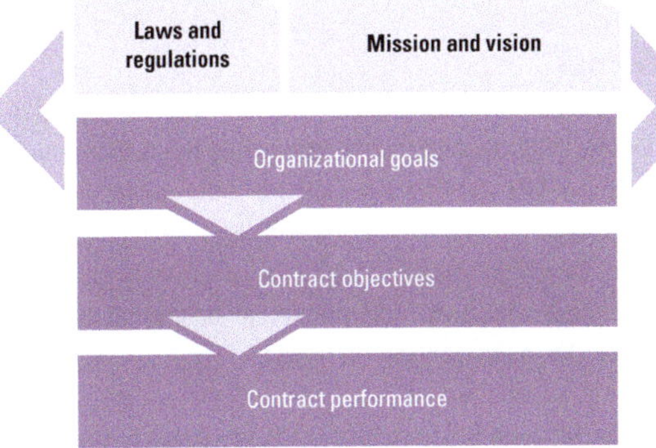

Figure 1: The relationship between organizational goals, contract objectives and contract performance

CATS CM® enables organizations to proactively manage contracts to optimize the realization of objectives. This is achieved by monitoring compliance with agreements, resolving uncertainties in a timely manner, managing risks, and, when necessary and possible, implementing desired changes in agreements. The CATS CM® methodology is suitable for both clients and suppliers.

In today's business environment, and in the public sector, organizations operate in a complex business ecosystem that is governed by a multitude of contracts that come with their own set of objectives, benefits and risks. CATS CM® offers a structured and scalable approach to contract management. It outlines the core principles, defines roles, and addresses key challenges for contract managers, providing clear guidance on effective practices. Additionally, it equips organizations with practical tools to implement contract management at both the policy and process levels.

3 SUMMARY

Contract management is defined as the realization of intended contract objectives by proactively monitoring the fulfillment of all contractually established responsibilities, obligations, procedures, agreements, conditions and rates, resolving all ambiguities, contradictions and white spaces, managing all contract-related risks, and implementing all desired changes to the contract, during the execution phase.

CATS CM® serves as a best practice framework, encompassing all activities required for effective contract management in the post-award phase of the contract lifecycle. Additionally, it establishes a foundation for determining the appropriate involvement during the pre-award phase of the lifecycle.

To translate the purpose and principles of contract management into actionable steps, CATS CM® introduces four pillars. These pillars provide clear and practical guidelines for defining and executing roles and responsibilities effectively. The roles involved are illustrated in figure 2.

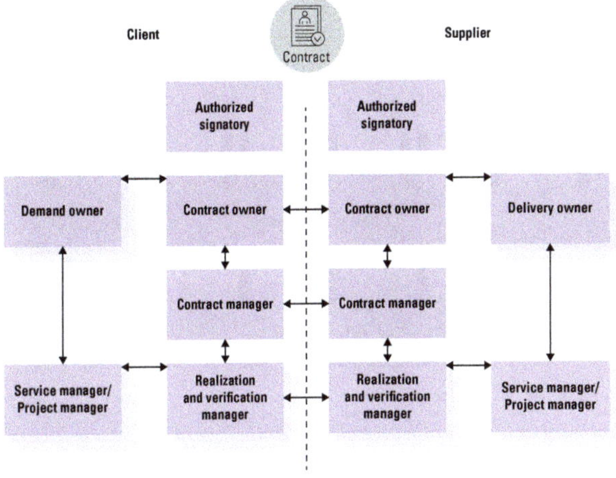

Figure 2: The roles that arise around the contract

Dividing the domain of contract management into smaller focus areas, Contract Management Essentials, allows users to scale their efforts and tailor their approach to the specific needs of a contract and the capabilities of the organization, figure 3.

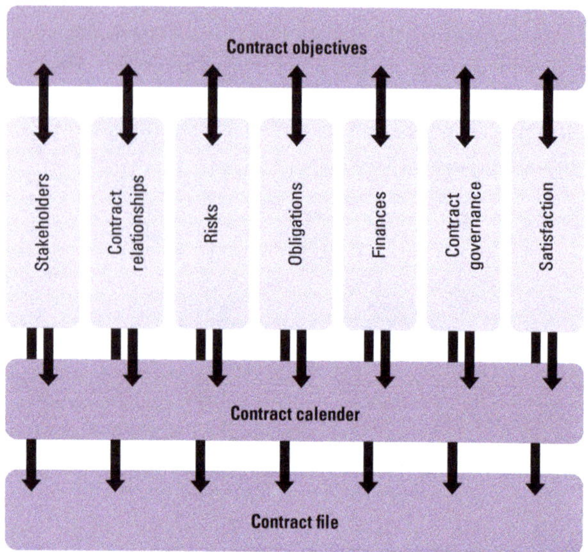

Figure 3: The ten CM Essentials

4 TARGET AUDIENCE

CATS CM® is designed for individuals, departments, and organizations aiming to maximize the added value of contracts in an efficient and effective manner. As such, this methodology is particularly relevant for:

- Contract managers involved in the day-to-day management of contracts on both the buyer's and seller's sides of organizations.
- Managers of contract management departments, responsible for overseeing contract management activities.
- Professionals involved in the pre-award phase of contracts (e.g., sales and procurement professionals) tasked with creating manageable and effective contracts.

- Service and project managers, who rely on contracts to deliver outcomes in their areas of responsibility.
- Contract owners, accountable for achieving the objectives tied to specific contracts.
- Process owners, CLM system suppliers, and consultants responsible for designing, optimizing, automating, and implementing contract management processes.

5 SCOPE AND CONSTRAINTS

CATS CM® focuses on managing and optimizing contracts during the contract execution phase. It considers all direct stakeholders of a contract and is specifically tailored for business-to-business contracts. While it can be partially applied to managing individual or small sets of contracts, its greatest value is realized when implemented across departments or organization wide.

CATS CM® complements several globally recognized standards for project management and service management. This relationship is further elaborated in the CATS RVM® methodology, which provides a detailed framework for linking existing service and project management methodologies with contract management practices based on CATS CM®.

6 RELEVANT WEBSITE

www.cats-cm.com

Contract Management with CATS CM® Version 4

Languages: English, Dutch

ISBN 9789401806862 (EN)

CATS CM® Foundation English - Exam

Language: English, Dutch

Product code VHLSCATSCMFEB (EN)

CATS RVM®

1 TITLE/ CURRENT VERSION

CATS RVM®

2 THE BASICS

When services or projects are linked to contracts, an interface emerges between service and project management on one side, and contract management on the other. This intersection is addressed through the domain of realization and verification management. The CATS RVM® methodology enables organizations to effectively integrate contract management into project and service management for both clients and suppliers.

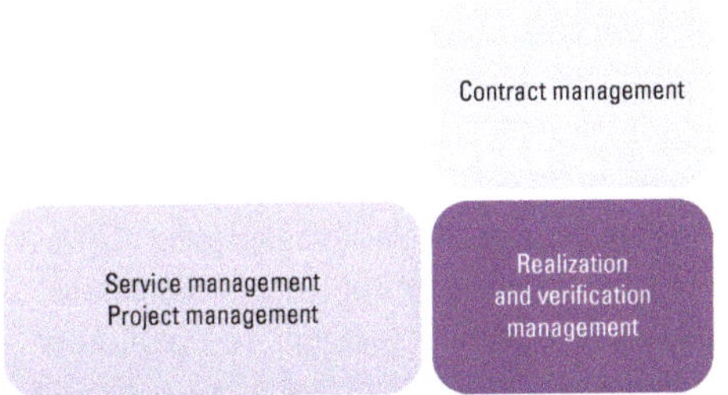

Figure 1: The domain of realization and verification management

The CATS RVM® methodology includes verifying performances, setting up delivery, risk management, establishing delivery processes, and aligning service and project management processes with the other party in a contract.
Introduced in 2022, CATS RVM® addresses the growing need to integrate contract management into an organization's operational processes. Contract management centers

on achieving contract objectives while aligning with an organization's mission, vision, and applicable laws and regulations. This methodology is based on the CATS CM® methodology that offers a proactive approach to managing contracts and optimizing the realization of objectives.

CATS RVM® offers a structured and scalable approach to managing contracts within the context of project and service management. It clearly outlines core principles, defines roles, and addresses key challenges for project managers, service managers, and comparable roles. Additionally, it provides practical tools and clear guidance to enhance effective practices across the organization.

3 SUMMARY

RVM stands for Realization and Verification Management, which forms the core of the methodology. Its focus lies on the realization and verification of contract performance, both as part of the organization's delivery and service or project management, and in relation to contract management. CATS RVM® serves as a best practice framework that encompasses all activities necessary for effective realization and verification management in the post-award phase of the contract lifecycle. Furthermore, it provides a foundation for determining the appropriate involvement during the pre-award phase.

To translate the purpose and principles of realization and verification management into actionable steps, CATS RVM® introduces four pillars. These pillars provide clear and practical guidance and tools for defining and executing roles and responsibilities effectively.

By dividing the domain of realization and verification into smaller focus areas, Realization and Verification Management Essentials, CATS RVM® allows users to scale their efforts and adapt their approach to the specific needs of a service or project, as well as the capabilities of the organization. The RVM Essentials align seamlessly with the Contract Management Essentials of the CATS CM® methodology and address common service and project management processes.

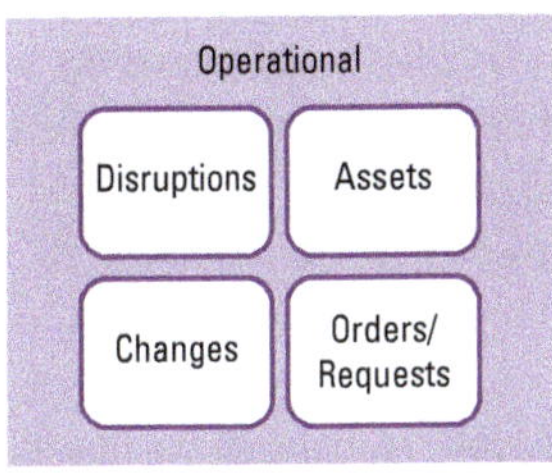

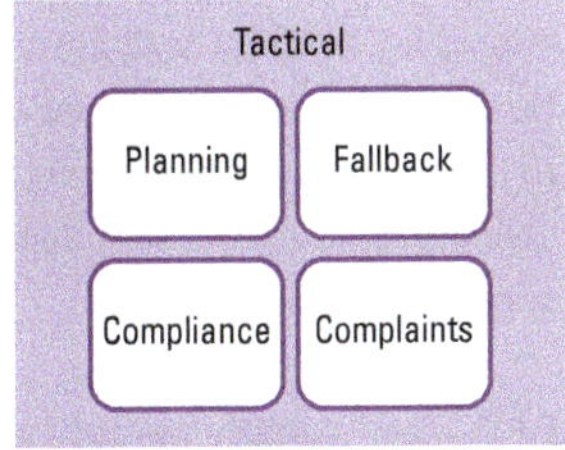

Figure 2: Service and project management processes included in the RVM Essentials

4 TARGET AUDIENCE

CATS RVM® is designed for individuals, departments, and organizations seeking to maximize the added value of contracts in an efficient and effective manner. This book is particularly valuable for:

- Service and project managers who are (partially) responsible for contract management or work in organizations that implement contract management based on the CATS CM® methodology.
- Contract managers interested in understanding the broader business impact of contracts.

- Managers of service or project management departments, responsible for overseeing contract management activities within projects and services.
- Contract owners, accountable for achieving the objectives associated with specific contracts.

5 SCOPE AND CONSTRAINTS

CATS RVM® focuses on managing and optimizing contracts in projects and services during the contract execution phase. It considers all direct stakeholders and is specifically tailored for business-to-business contracts. While it can be partially applied to managing individual or small sets of contracts, its greatest value is realized when implemented across departments or organization wide.

CATS RVM® complements several globally recognized standards for project management and service management.

6 RELEVANT WEBSITE

www.cats-cm.com

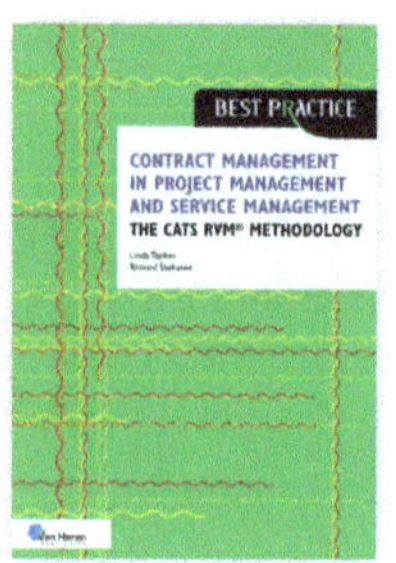

Contract Management in Project Management and Service Management – The CATS RVM® Methodology

Languages: English, Dutch

ISBN 9789401810487 (EN)

Growth Hacking

1 TITLE/ CURRENT VERSION

Growth Hacking is a driver for continuous value creation.

2 THE BASICS

As the person responsible for growth in your business today, what you need is a new, more dynamic approach. An approach that understands different perspectives in the customer journey and the synergies between different ways of working: growing from marketing, sales and/or product.

Structurally discovering, developing, and launching new propositions aligned with your vision, is essential in these times. This requires ideas. Ideas for new propositions, but perhaps more importantly, for the further development of your existing products and services.

And, to get from idea to scalable, sustainable growth as quickly as possible – you also need a sustainable and methodical approach. This domain and this approach are what we call Continuous Value Creation. This approach will be at the core of the Masters of Growth certification program.

3 SUMMARY

Complex, rapidly changing and highly specialized. This is the world we're operating in at the moment. Marketing, product development and innovation are becoming more and more challenging for business leaders. Customer journeys are becoming more complex. The number of available and necessary tools for managing marketing, product, activation, and retention is growing exponentially. How do you maintain the helicopter overview in this ocean of tools and processes? And more importantly, how do you keep focusing on what you need to be focusing on?

Growth and the continuous creation of value consist of two important phases: the Idea Phase and the Growth Phase. Design Thinking and Growth Hacking are the methods you use to achieve scalable growth in the specific phases of this growth cycle.

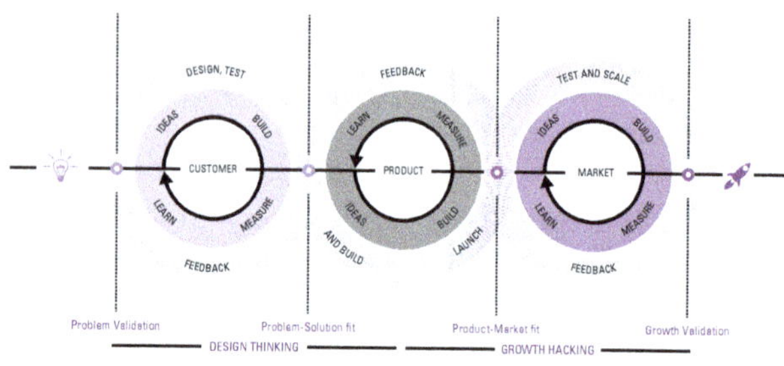

Design Thinking is what you focus on in the Idea Phase: in service of designing a proposition by discovering customer value (based on a validated problem or need). While Growth Hacking is about accelerating growth; catalyzing and improving value (where possible, very quickly) into a scalable proposition. Both have equally important roles as they complement each other on the road towards growth. Feedback is the artery through which the continuous flow of insights contributes to the process of value creation.

4 TARGET AUDIENCE

The Masters of Growth course is a certification program for all professionals involved in growth in business. It will teach those responsible for Growth all of the necessary strategies, tactics and tools they need to implement the above framework. As the

end result, you will be able to act at a strategic level, to plan and translate this all the way down to execution across the entire spectrum of growth within your organization. From finance to product, from sales to marketing, with maximum, sustainable growth as a result. Specific roles for whom we expect the certification to add a lot of value are:

- Product Managers/Owners
- Product Developers/UX Designers
- Marketing Managers
- CCOs, CMOs
- Sales Reps

5 RELEVANT READING

Read more about Growth hacking and Continuous Value Creation:

https://blog.bammboo.io/en/growth-hacking-as-a-driver-for-sustainable-growth/

MOG - Growth Hacking Foundation Courseware

Languages: English,

ISBN 9789401809467 (EN)

MOG - Growth Hacking Foundation - Exam

Language: English

Product code GROWTHMASTERB

Lean Six Sigma

1 TITLE/ CURRENT VERSION

Lean Six Sigma

2 THE BASICS

Lean Six Sigma is a coming together of both Lean Management and Six Sigma. Lean Management is best defined as "a management philosophy focused on identifying and eliminating waste throughout an entire value stream, extending not only within the organization, but also along its entire supply chain network". Six Sigma is best defined as "an organized and systematic methodology for strategic process improvement and new product and service development that relies on statistical methods and the scientific method to make dramatic reductions in customer defined defect rates". Together Lean Six Sigma can best be defined as "a structured data-based approach for sustainable process improvement".

3 SUMMARY

Lean Six Sigma is the global standard for organizing the design, data-based improvement and control of both manual and digital business processes. Well-designed and controlled processes are key in achieving and sustaining operational excellence. They ensure the quality of service and care, the reliability and safety of work that is done, and a timely processing with short waiting times. High quality processes will at the same time improve the operation's flexibility. Thereby allowing one to adjust to changes in demand and other circumstances. An organizational capability to harness data-based process improvement, finally, facilitates organizational learning and is foundational for the

fruitful implementation of ever-increasing digitization and automation opportunities.

Lean Six Sigma offers a complete model for shaping modern continuous improvement programs in organizations. The methodology is built on principles and methods for fact-based process improvement that have proven themselves over the last decades, and will continue to do so in the decades to come. Having emerged in manufacturing, the approach continuously evolved and gained tremendous momentum in other industries (e.g. services, healthcare, public administration, education, etc.).

Core principles of the Lean Six Sigma methodology:
1. Professional and science-based problem solving
2. Precise, quantitative and business case-based problem definition
3. Data-based diagnosis
4. Innovative generation of new ideas and solutions
5. Field-testing of ideas before implementation
6. Proven sustainable improvement realization

The DMAIC roadmap

The principles outlined above are operationalized by the DMAIC roadmap. It employs five phases: Define (D), Measure (M), Analyze (A), Improve (I) and Control (C). The roadmap guides, helps in asking the right questions, prescribes when certain tools and techniques can be used, and forces to organize findings in a structured manner.
1. Define: Select project and project lead and establish objectives and conditions
2. Measure: Make the problem quantifiable and measurable
3. Analyze: Analyze the current situation and make a diagnosis
4. Improve: Develop and implement improvement actions

5. Control: Adjust the quality control system and close the project

4 TARGET AUDIENCE

Managers and professionals that have business improvement as core responsibility and interest:

- Operational Excellence professionals (a.o. Lean Six Sigma Green and Black Belts); effectively improving processes and organizational problems is a full-time dedication in many organizations nowadays. Mastering the comprehensive Lean Six Sigma methodology is a prerequisite for adequately doing so.
- Process and project managers; evidence-based, data driven, and sustainable process improvement is vital for the well-functioning of any organizational domain, regardless of sector or industry. Having a profound understanding of the concepts for doing so is regarded a 21st century prerequisite to be effective in change-oriented business functions.
- Business and senior managers; regardless of their functional focus, the ability to recognize, install and lead process improvement initiatives is vital for continuous improvement and ongoing business innovation.
- Other managers and professionals; everyone within an organization that is confronted with processes, the problems that can emerge there, or the ineffective execution of these processes.

5 SCOPE AND CONSTRAINTS

The premier focus of Lean Six Sigma is to improve operational performance by improving repetitive processes. Thereby Lean Six Sigma is unique, but not without complementarity.

1. First, the capability to understand and sustainably improve processes allows for optimal decision-making related

to process automation opportunities, optimal design of business intelligence monitoring solutions and effective deployment of data science capabilities.

2. Second, Lean Six Sigma is a comprehensive methodology that enables business process management in organizations. It provides powerful instruments and guidelines for process owners to, besides manage, optimize processes.
3. Finally, Lean Six Sigma is a methodology (i.e. a collection of principles and powerful (statistical) techniques to make data-based decisions) that are traditionally deployed in structured project formats. For a methodology to be accepted and adopted, appropriate deployment structures that fit existing organizational ways-of-working should be designed, either more or less iterative (e.g. Agile Scrum) or collaborative.

6 RELEVANT WEBSITES

Lean Six Sigma International Association of Professionals – https://lssiap.co.uk/
American Society for Quality – https://asq.org/
University of Amsterdam Institute for Business and Industrial Statistics (IBIS UvA) – https://ibisuva.nl/

Lean Six Sigma Green Belt
Languages: English, Dutch

ISBN 9789401809733 (EN)

LSSA Lean (Six Sigma)- Green Belt Courseware
Language: English

ISBN 9789401810678

OBM

1 TITLE/ CURRENT VERSION

OBM (Organizational Behavior Management).

2 THE BASICS

OBM is a scientifically proven method for optimizing organizational performance by combining a 6-step protocol with hard data and a focus on positive change. Used successfully worldwide for over 40 years, OBM has a proven track record of improving organizational performance in every field of business, in hundreds of reported cases. Based on the behavioral science called Applied Behavior Analysis, OBM is the application of this science in organizational settings. OBM is targeted to measurably improve performance by focusing on behavior instead of just results. By this it takes a positive stance towards the design and implementation of organizational change. It also helps leaders recognize and avoid the three common pitfalls of behavioral influence, making current leadership only effective in a mere 0.8% of their efforts of changing behavior.

3 SUMMARY

The facts are both confrontational and undeniable. For decades repeated research by e.g. McKinsey has shown that a staggering 70% of organizational change programs fail to meet all their objectives. In no less than 60% of those cases 'behavior' is determined as the root cause. That is, a failure to get people to actually DO the things that the program aimed for.
Three major frustrations in boardrooms concerning behavioral change in organizations are:

1. Why don't they do what we agreed upon?

2. Why do our behavioral interventions not work out in a sustainable way?
3. How do we get them to do it anyway?

OBM offers solutions from modern business administration with all the answers. In a nutshell:

- OBM is both a practical and scientific approach to organizational behavior change
- It is an evidence-based, fact-driven method
- OBM has its roots in the U.S. and has been taught for decades at universities worldwide
- It is increasingly being called 'the Science of Success' because OBM has proven to measurably optimize business performances for hundreds of times, in very diverse situations
- OBM can be seamlessly integrated with other methods and frameworks e.g. Lean, Six Sigma, ITIL, Agile, Scrum, etc. and it increases their effects
- With OBM one can measurably and noticeably increase performances and, when properly applied, can bring out the best in people with sustained effect
- Since the 1970s OBM has bridged the gap between behavioral sciences and business administration through the use of a performance improvement protocol. Every step of that protocol is an important ingredient of the medicine
- Where many other methods stop at the definition of goals, KPIs and individual targets, OBM takes it one essential step further: In OBM behavior is made measurable. In the end it is all about what people really DO to make an actual contribution to a target or not

- At its foundation lies a positive approach in which desired organizational behaviors are reinforced as much as possible by applying positive consequences
- The focus is on catching people doing the right things, instead of only criticizing non-compliance or underachievement. Reinforcing behavior through recognition increases the probability that the behavior will occur again because of a bio-chemical process in the brain

As one of the key founders of OBM, Aubrey Daniels PhD puts it: "People love change! As long as they benefit from it themselves." A fact often forgotten to take into account when designing and implementing organizational change, since in most cases only the organizational benefits are defined.
Where many frameworks provide business leaders with structures pertaining to the WHY and WHAT, OBM is mostly concerned with the HOW of organizational change. OBM consists of a scientifically proven 6-step protocol:

1. Specify Performance in terms of both desired results and underlying behaviors
2. Design, implement and use a Performance Measurement system to establish (changes in) levels of performance and the gap between end goal and current performance
3. Analyze both current unwanted behaviors and desired behaviors using the ABC-analysis
4. Organize effective Feedback in both a graphically and verbally appealing way
5. Set Sub goals to divide the gap between end goal and current performance in acceptable and attainable steps
6. Give Rewards for attaining goals and – most of all – Recognition for displaying the desired behaviors leading to the results connected to those goals

4 TARGET AUDIENCE

OBM is interesting for anyone who is responsible for achieving goals that are 'bigger than them', i.e. they need others in order to be able to attain them and need to influence their performances. The higher up the organization it is embedded and cascaded down the chain of command, the more successful it can become.
Users include:

- Leaders and managers at all levels
- Business consultants
- IT consultants
- Security consultants
- Project managers
- Occupational safety consultants
- Executive coaches

5 SCOPE AND CONSTRAINTS

While relatively easy to understand, based on simple concepts and being extremely powerful if applied correctly, the proper use of OBM needs time to settle in the behavior of leaders themselves. Sometimes cheerfully compared to a dog training, the important thing is to realize who's being trained in these canine competence exercises: Indeed, the owner of the dog, not the dog itself!
It is therefore the behavior of the leader that reciprocates into the desired behavior of the follower. OBM can therefore also be seen as a way to hone leadership skills.

Strengths

- Scientifically proven method, based on decades of corroborative research in both laboratory settings and experimental case studies

- Evidenced based
- Making behavior measurable
- Focus on positive change
- Making use of biochemical processes in the brain

Constraints

- The method needs to be taught as well as experienced in a live case by influencers before further successful application
- For full performance yields a top-down approach is favorable
- Leaders must be ready to change their own behaviors as well, or at least accept it as a necessary step
- Reciprocity can induce both an upward or downward relationship spiral. You get what you reinforce (!)

6 RECOMMENDED READING

Aubrey C. Daniels & Jon S. Bailey, *Performance Management: Changing Behavior that Drives Organizational Effectiveness*, 5th Edition, 2014, Atlanta
www.adriba.vu.nl

Organizational Behavior Management – An Introduction

Language: English Dutch and German

ISBN 9789401807074

The courseware for the OBM Dynamics – OBM Foundation Level examiniation

Language: English, Dutch, German

ISBN 9789401809528

OPBOK

1 TITLE/ CURRENT VERSION

OPBOK (Outsourcing Professional Body of Knowledge)
Version 10

2 THE BASICS

OPBOK (Outsourcing Professional Body of Knowledge) provides a set of best practices from around the globe for the design, implementation and management of outsourcing contracts, including a code of ethics and business practices for outsourcing professionals.

3 SUMMARY

OPBOK (Outsourcing Professional Body of Knowledge) is owned and maintained by the International Association of Outsourcing Professionals (IAOP). which was formed in 2005 by a consortium of leading companies involved in outsourcing as customers, providers, and advisors. OPBOK was first published in 2006; the current version is Version 10, which reflects major updates from IAOP of the commonly accepted practices and skills required to ensure outsourcing success. It is the basis for IAOP's Certified Outsourcing Professional® qualification and certification programmes.

OPBOK describes the generally accepted set of knowledge and practices applicable to the successful design, implementation, and management of outsourcing contracts. It provides:

- A framework for understanding what outsourcing is and how it fits within business operations
- The knowledge and practice areas generally accepted as critical to outsourcing success

- A glossary of terms commonly used in outsourcing deals and contracts

OPBOK is divided into ten knowledge areas covering major areas of outsourcing expertise. The OPBOK framework is based on a five-stage outsourcing process (see Figure).

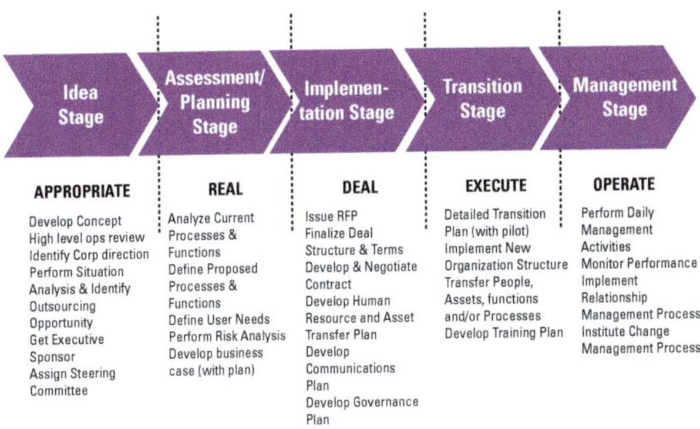

Figure: OPBOK five stage outsourcing process (Source IAOP)

4 TARGET AUDIENCE

Targeted principally at outsourcing professionals who are buyers, providers and advisors in the outsourcing industry; also of interest to senior management in buying organizations; trainers and academics addressing outsourcing topics.

5 SCOPE AND CONSTRAINTS

The scope of OPBOK is governance and defining a strategic approach to outsourcing, governance, identifying and communicating business requirements, selecting and qualifying providers, gaining internal buy-in, creating project teams, and getting value for money and return on investment. OPBOK and

Carnegie Mellon's eSourcing Capability Models (eSCMs) are becoming the most relevant outsourcing standards. OPBOK complements eSCM-CL (eSCM for clients). OPBOK focuses on outsourcing of any service (but only outsourcing). eSCM-CL focuses on sourcing of IT-enabled services and covers multiple types of sourcing, including outsourcing, insourcing, and shared services. OPBOK is used as the basis for individual certification – the Certified Outsourcing Professional (COP), while eSCM-CL supports organizational appraisal, evaluation, and certification.

Strengths
OPBOK reflects the best practice of outsourcing professionals worldwide, including the 'make or break' factors that can affect any outsourcing initiative.

Constraints
OPBOK does not address insourcing or shared services.

6 RELEVANT WEBSITE

www.iaop.org

Outsourcing Professional Body of Knowledge
Language: English

ISBN 9789401800006

Operating Model Canvas

1 TITLE/ CURRENT VERSION

Operating Model Canvas: Aligning operations and organization with strategy

2 THE BASICS

Operating Model Canvas describes a tool that managers can use to help them achieve alignment with strategy and with each other. It presents many examples from Uber to Shell to an IT function to a charity. It includes a toolbox of nearly 20 tools that help analyse and define an operating model. It also has two fully worked case studies.

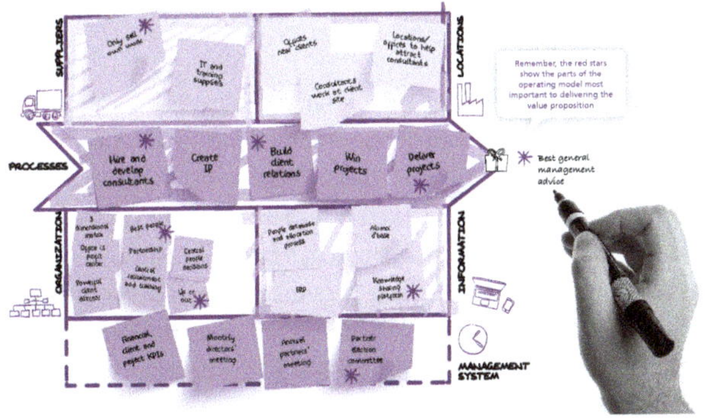

The Operating Model Canvas dovetails with the Business Model Canvas. As Yves Pigneur, author of Business Model Generation and Value Proposition Design explains "Andrew Campbell and co-authors have focused on the left-hand side of the Business Model Canvas for creating an Operating Model Canvas." Patrick van der Pijl, author of Design a Better Business added "This book is part of a family of books – Business Model Generation, Value

Proposition Design and Design a better Business. They should all be in your bookshelf or on the side of your desk."

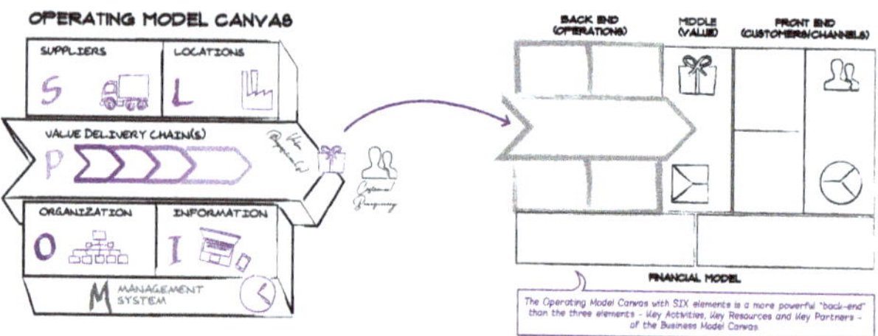

3 SUMMARY

An operating model is a document. It helps high level management to convert strategy into operational implications. Think of a building blueprint.

An operating model helps senior managers make operational choices. It helps the head of operations design the detailed work processes. It helps the head of HR decide what sort of people are needed to do the work and what sort of structure is needed to guide and control them. It helps the head of IT make decisions about IT architecture. It helps the head of supply chain design relationships with suppliers. So an operating model is an important step between strategy and all the decisions that need to be made to create a functioning organization.

A high-level operating model can be a single page. Of course there are operating models of 100 pages and operating manuals of more than 1000 pages. Though this book is about high-level models.

The Operating Model Canvas is a one-page model. For those familiar with the Business Model Canvas, the Operating Model Canvas covers the operating elements (Activities, Resources and Partners) with six elements that make up the mnemonic POLISM – Processes, Organization, Locations, Information, Suppliers and Management system.

Processes for the work that needs to be done to deliver a value proposition or service proposition to a customer/beneficiary: the value delivery chain. Organization for people who will do the work, the structure, the functions needed to support the work and the decision powers given to people in the structure. Location for where the work is done. Information for the software applications needed to support the work. Suppliers for those outside the organization whose engagement is also needed. Management system for planning, budgeting, performance monitoring and controls needed to run the organization.

It is possible to create an Operating Model Canvas for a multinational company, for a single business, for a function like HR or sales within a business, for a department within a function, for a charity and for a government body.

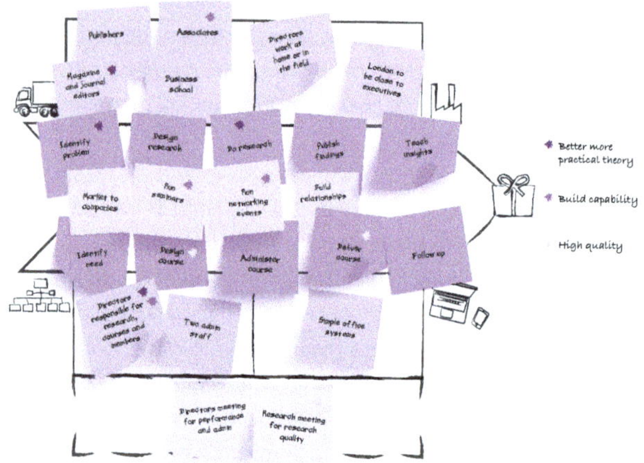

The book shows you how to create an Operating Model Canvas and provides dozens of examples of all different types of Canvases.

Chapter 1 - Operating Model Canvas
Describes the link with the Business Model Canvas and the role that an Operating Model Canvas plays in a transformation journey

Chapter 2 - Operating Model Canvas examples
15 examples of real organizations from Uber to Shell to an IT function to Cardboard Citizens

Chapter 3 - Toolbox
18 tools divided between 5 core tools and 13 additional tools

Chapter 4 - Designing a target operating model for a business
Fully worked example of a company in the business of supplying equipment to the electricity transmission industry

Chapter 5 – Designing an operating model for a function

Fully worked example of an IT function

Chapter 6 – Change examples

Six 'as is' and 'to be' examples that improved performance

4 TARGET AUDIENCE

- A manager in operations or in any function who wants to design how the operation works
- A CEO or COO or entrepreneur who wants to review his or her organization and plans
- A lean practitioner or process excellence manager who wants to be more strategic
- A manager in strategy or planning who wants to make the plans more practical
- A project manager or change specialist working on a transformation project
- A leader who wants to make sure her team members are all on the same page
- A business partner in HR, IT or Finance who wants to improve the business
- A business development manager who wants to design a new business
- A Business Architect, Enterprise Architect or Operations Strategist
- A manager tasked with cutting costs or improving service or quality
- A customer experience or user experience specialist
- A manager in charge of post merger integration
- A consultant helping organizations improve
- Anyone responsible for performance

5 SCOPE

- What is an operating model?
- The link between operating models and business models
- The link between operating models and strategy
- The tools of operating model design
- How to design a target operating model
- Fully worked examples of operating model design
- The role of an operating model in transformation

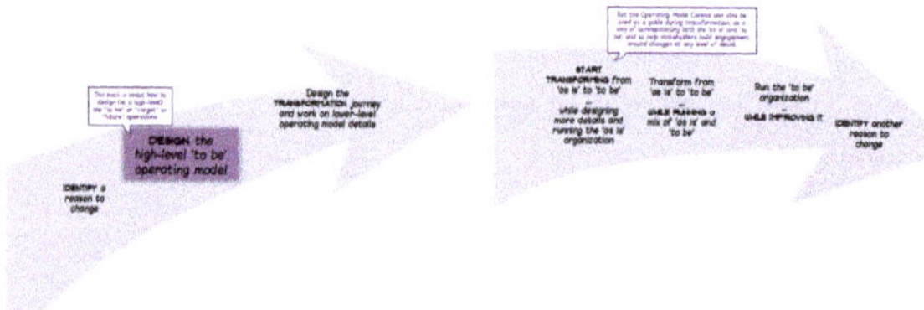

6 RELEVANT WEBSITE

https://operatingmodelcanvas.com/

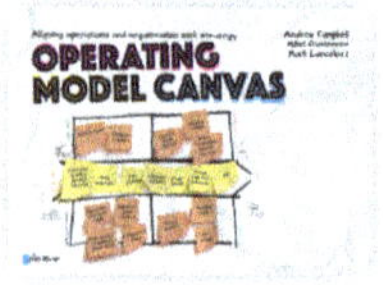

Operating Model Canvas

Languages: English, Chinese

ISBN 9789401800716 (EN)

RASCI method™

1 TITLE/CURRENT VERSION

The RASCI method™ and the RASCI model™.

2 THE BASICS

The RASCI method is a participative approach that is used to stimulate organizations in process-oriented thinking and working. The approach provides a structure that has been proven in practice as well as a concrete step-by-step plan for the development and optimization of processes and responsibilities. In addition to the representation via the RASCI model (Figure 1), a specified framework, 3-2-1 approach and 8-Step plan are used (Figure 2).

Characteristic is that those involved in the organization enter a dialogue with each other in a participative manner, while they are professionally facilitated. It's a step-by-step process that leads to a supported outcome that is guaranteed to meet the frameworks set in advance by management.

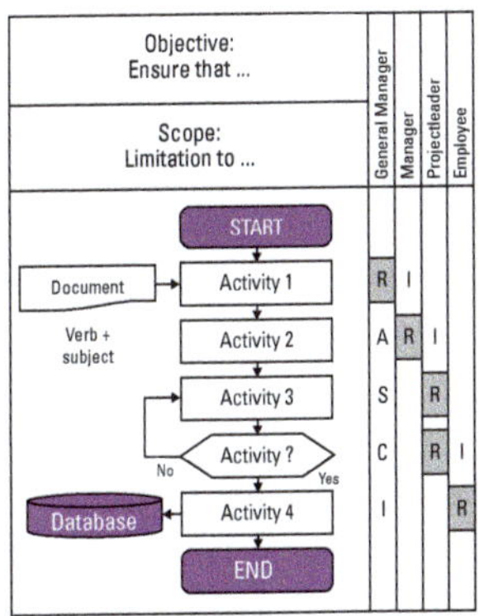

Figure 1: The RASCI model: Process and responsibilities powerfully combined.

What does RASCI mean?
RASCI® is an acronym, where the letters stand for the different roles that people can have in a process. Responsible, Accountable, Supporting, Consulted and Informed.

3 SUMMARY

The RASCI method works from the conviction that there is more potential in every organization and that you can achieve whatever you want with the right people at the table.
Based on years of experience with process management, the RASCI-method has been developed and repeatedly refined. It allows organizations to be facilitated with the desired change in a professional manner. The change process is facilitated by qualified consultants who guide managers, process owners and employees with the desired change.
In this way, process-oriented thinking and working are stimulated in organizations:

- By starting from Rhineland principles in which craftsmanship, trust and connection are central values.
- By combining expertise in the field of risk management, process management and improvement management.
- By giving employees a key role in implementing change, so that the change is not imposed but achieved from within.

In this way, the collective intelligence within the organization is activated and people are facilitated and activated to do what is required.

Management determines the strategic direction and starting points through the strategic objectives and frameworks to be used. To achieve the strategic objectives, it is assessed whether the current business model is still appropriate.

Through multidisciplinary teams, both the business model and the processes are assessed, aligned, and improved at a detailed level. Qualified consultants facilitate these interactive sessions in which ownership and the desired working method are determined and implemented within the organization concerned. This creates an effective and efficient working method that fits the chosen strategic direction. In this way, the available knowledge and experience at all levels are optimally connected and deployed (Figure 2).

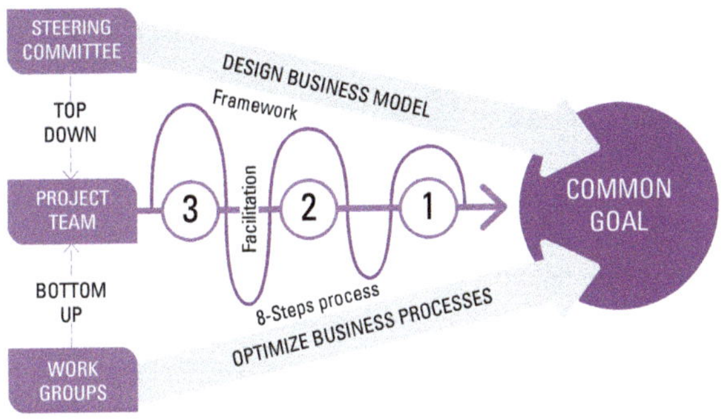

Figure 2: The RASCI method: Connection between strategy and operation.

The business model

All the processes required to realize the organization's strategy are reflected in the business model. This should include the management, support, primary and improvement processes. It provides everyone inside and outside the organization a complete overview of all processes and their interdependence.

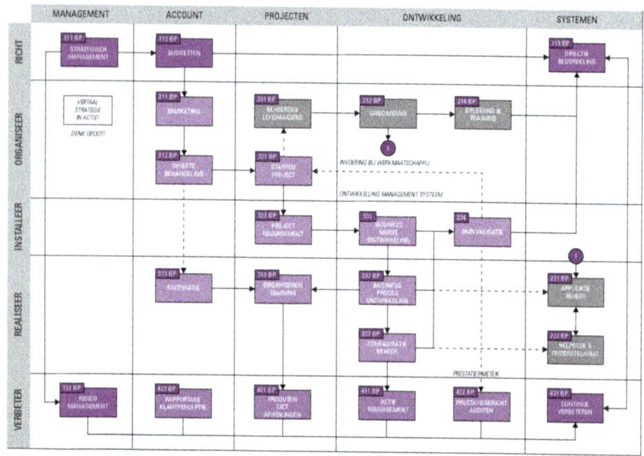

Figure 3: The business model.

The RASCI model

The RASCI model (Figure 1) combines in a compact way the description of a business process with the responsibilities associated for each step. For each business process, one page shows the objective, the scope and all the required activities and decisions to achieve the relevant goal. The corresponding RASCI roles are defined for each step in the same overview, so that it is clear at a glance to all involved how they should work together to achieve the desired result.

4 TARGET AUDIENCE

The RASCI method can be used wherever people work together to achieve a common goal and can be applied in any type of organization.

Typical users of the RASCI method are:

- Leaders and managers at all levels.

- Process Managers and Process Owners.
- QHSE managers (quality, health, safety and environment).
- Information security consultants (ISMS).
- Internal and external facilitators of change processes.
- Everyone involved in modeling and improving processes.
- Everyone involved in the development and implementation of management systems.
- Organizational consultants and trainers.
- Students and trainees, public administration and business economics.

5 SCOPE AND CONSTRAINTS

By means of the RASCI method, a systematic connection is made between the strategy of the organization, the associated business model, and the design of the relevant business processes. Due to the participative way of working, the result is supported by all involved and the desired change starts immediately.

Strengths

- Concise and understandable presentation of business processes.
- Clarity about the desired working method.
- Clarity in tasks, responsibilities, and authorities.
- Broad support for the required change.
- Respond faster to changing circumstances.
- Improved cooperation between employees of different departments.
- Insight into the relations between the business processes.
- Easily comply with international standards such as: ISO 9001 (quality management), ISO 14001 (environment), ISO 45001 (security management) and ISO 27001 (information security management).

Constraints

While the RASCI method is easy to understand and based on simple principles making it extremely powerful when used correctly, proper application of the RASCI method is also critical.

- The RASCI method should be well taught, supervised and experienced in practice for optimal application and acceptance within the organization.
- For maximum effect, a top-down and bottom-up approach should be applied simultaneously to ensure that strategy and operations come together in the right way.
- It is essential to involve the right people at the right time in every business process. Both on a management, tactical as well as on an operational level.
- All those involved should receive training in advance to make them aware of the different roles and responsibilities they will have when applying the RASCI method.
- Top management must be prepared and able to steer from frameworks.

6 RELEVANT WEBSITES

Information platform: RASCI.net – www.rasci.net (Dutch and English)
Consultancy and training: RASCI Methode B.V. – www.rascimethode.nl (Dutch and English)

RASCI-methode – Bedrijfsprocessen én verantwoordelijkheden kernachtig in kaart
Language: Dutch

ISBN 9789401810951

Thoughtleader Development Model

1. TITLE/CURRENT VERSION

Thoughtleader Development Model: Cultivating thought leadership, the content-powered approach to personal and organizational growth.

2. THE BASICS

The Thoughtleader Development Model guides readers and organizations to make more impact from their ideas, by growing their capabilities in five different domains. This enables them to expand on their thoughts, grow their network and accelerate their careers and revenue growth.

3. SUMMARY

The TDM model describes the journey of how to grow from an expert to a real thoughtleader. After defining the characteristics of a 'thoughtleader', the model gives insight in five elements that thoughtleaders need to process:

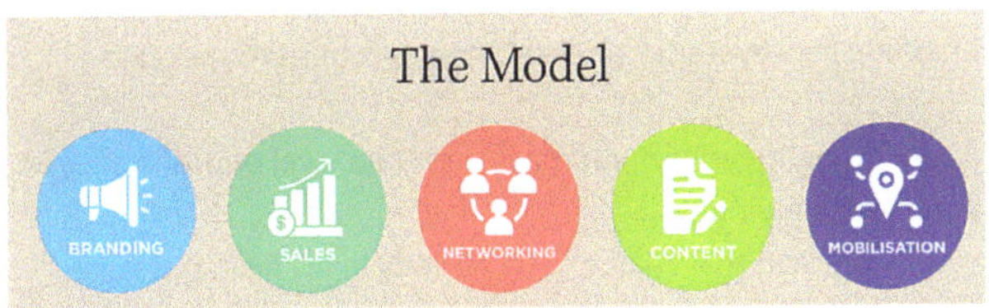

Content creation

The ability to generate forward-looking content that is contextualized broadly and, if possible, incites discussion to foster engagement and progression.

Networking and knowledge gathering

The process of acquiring knowledge as part of the thought leadership journey, alongside the capability to build a network to disseminate one's ideas.

Personal branding

Crafting a recognizable personal brand in the market to be regarded as a sought-after thought leader.

Salesmanship

The competence to market oneself, one's ideas, and one's organization. Many thought leaders are integral parts of larger entities and must effectively promote the organization's offerings and products. Their role involves positioning the organization at the forefront when it comes to sales. Therefore, advocating for deals or assisting the sales team in closing deals is a vital aspect of thought leadership.

Influence and support (mobilization)

The critical ability to garner support from others, ensuring that one's ideas gain traction and receive the necessary backing, particularly when challenges arise (including political ones), enabling perseverance and securing appropriate support.

Every thoughtleader must reach a certain level of proficiency in each of the elements:

- A Craftsman that is an expert already in his field, but very specialized and very much in-depth focused on his/her level of expertise itself.
- An Advisor to others on the specific topic of his/her field. Knows to contextualize the topic considering all other developments ongoing (economical, technological, etc.).

- A Visionaire that will give prediction on the future based on one's topic. Will be able to describe a 'Horizon 3' and can explain what the implication on the short and mid-term are as well as the long term.

The second part of the model argues that you not only need to reach a certain proficiency level, but that true thoughtleaders are a Visionaire on at least one, an advisor on one other element and need to be at least a Craftsman on the other three elements

The model describes the different levels of proficiency for each of the elements, gives examples of rolemodels to draw inspiration from and gives examples and exercises to increase one's proficiency.

4. TARGET AUDIENCE

There is a wide range of professionals that can benefit from developing their thoughtleader capabilities, e.g. consultants who want to increase their influence at their clients. Or where it is young professionals who wants to kickstart their career or seasoned consultants who still want to take their next step.

Sales professionals will benefit in increasing their ability to find the right stakeholders at their clients as well as having the right dialogue from a content perspective, thereby increasing their credibility with the client.

It is also a useful tool for managers to give more guidance to their people on lead by example. This is by no means a complete list. The different trainings on this model were attended by project managers, delivery managers, sales managers and operational managers, who all have given the feedback that the model has increased their ability to take more ownership of their ideas and their organization's destiny.

5. SCOPE

The TDM model gives insight in how you can grow as a company through exposing the intellect that is present in your organization in a better and more professional way to your clients. As an individual it will give you the ability to grow your career, but also increase your own circle of influence and enlarge your systematic thinking on your 'thought'.

6. RELEVANT WEBSITES

https://www.thoughtleaderdevelopment.com/
https://www.thoughtleaderdevelopment.nl/

www.ingramcontent.com/pod-product-compliance
Ingram Content Group UK Ltd.
Pitfield, Milton Keynes, MK11 3LW, UK
UKHW021826270726
14058UKWH00001B/1

9 789401 813099